BLUE Monday

THE EXPOS, THE DODGERS,

AND THE HOME RUN THAT CHANGED EVERYTHING

DANNY GALLAGHER

FOREWORD BY LARRY PARRISH

DUNDURN

TORONTO

Cover design: Ron Beltrame
Printer: Webcom

Library and Archives Canada Cataloguing in Publication

Gallagher, Danny, 1950-, author
    Blue Monday : the Expos, the Dodgers, and the home
run that changed everything / Danny Gallagher; foreword by Larry Parrish.

Includes bibliographical references and index.
Issued in print and electronic formats.
ISBN 978-1-4597-4187-4 (softcover).--ISBN 978-1-4597-4188-1
(PDF).--ISBN 978-1-4597-4189-8 (EPUB)

    1. Baseball--United States--History--20th century. 2. Home runs
(Baseball). 3. Monday, Rick, 1945-. 4. Rogers, Steve, 1949-. 5. Montreal Expos
(Baseball team)--History. 6. Los Angeles Dodgers (Baseball team)--History. I. Title.

GV868.4.G35 2018   796.3570973'09048   C2018-903354-1
                                                          C2018-903355-X

1 2 3 4 5   22 21 20 19 18

We acknowledge the support of the **Canada Council for the Arts**, which last year invested $153 million to bring the arts to Canadians throughout the country, and the **Ontario Arts Council** for our publishing program. We also acknowledge the financial support of the **Government of Ontario**, through the **Ontario Book Publishing Tax Credit** and the **Ontario Media Development Corporation**, and the **Government of Canada**.

Nous remercions le **Conseil des arts du Canada** de son soutien. L'an dernier, le Conseil a investi 153 millions de dollars pour mettre de l'art dans la vie des Canadiennes et des Canadiens de tout le pays.

Care has been taken to trace the ownership of copyright material used in this book. The author and the publisher welcome any information enabling them to rectify any references or credits in subsequent editions.
— *J. Kirk Howard, President*

The publisher is not responsible for websites or their content unless they are owned by the publisher.

Printed and bound in Canada.

VISIT US AT

 dundurn.com | @dundurnpress | dundurnpress | dundurnpress

Dundurn
3 Church Street, Suite 500
Toronto, Ontario, Canada
M5E 1M2

To Gerry Snyder, Charles Bronfman, John McHale, Jim Fanning, and Harry Renaud, five instrumental figures in the formation of the Expos. Most people know who Bronfman, McHale, and Fanning are, but Snyder and Renaud probably need some explanation. Snyder was the Montreal city councillor who spent a lot of time attending National League meetings and lobbying team owners in the 1960s about the merits of baseball in Montreal. He doesn't get enough credit for Montreal's success in obtaining a franchise in May of 1968. Renaud was the team's secretary-treasurer and CFO from day one through to July of 1981.

CONTENTS

Foreword

Hi folks, this is L.P. This book of Danny's covers the late 1970s leading up to the 1981 season, which includes Blue Monday. It covers the plots and subplots that every team goes through to reach their goal. In your life, when things are happening, you aren't aware a lot of times how important the event you are going through affects your life and the people around you.

I know that I was raised in a small town in the South, and without baseball I never would have experienced the community and culture of a city like Montreal. I know I was affected by a couple of "Mels," and their memories will still be a part of Expos history.

The first Mel was Mel Didier. He was the Expos' farm system director in the early 1970s. I know he was the reason I signed with Montreal. He was baseball through and through. I can still remember him giving us a talk when we all got together after the 1972 draft. He used the word *podnuh* (partner) a lot, and I remember him saying, "Podnuh, I'm going to look you eyeball to eyeball and belly button to belly button." And he was always true to those words.

The second Mel was Mel Yas. He and his wife Shirley had great hearts and helped a lot of young men and their families when they came to

Montreal. They drove you around and helped you look for living quarters and just aided so many Expos in the 1970s.

I remember the different men I played with. A baseball team is made up of people from so many backgrounds — people from Latin America, the United States, Canada, Japan, and throughout the world. How they get along, learn from each other, and strive for one goal is a pretty good lesson in life.

Then, here in the United States, we had inner-city kids linked together with some kids from the South. It seems like a big difference, but when you get to know each other, you realize people are just the same. I know — because I am one of those kids. I started my career with Ellis Valentine. He was a high draft pick out of the Los Angeles area and I was a small-town kid from the South, but as we played together and I got to know his parents and he got to know mine, over the years, we formed a bond that is still there today.

You know, you remember that we had some great players with the Expos. We had Hall of Famers. We had the Kid, the Hawk, and Rock. But we also had Cy, Doggie, Cro, Cool Breeze, Waxo, Gully, Scotty, Eli, and, of course, the Spaceman. All of these guys were pretty darn good, too.

As you can tell, I do love reliving those days. Hopefully, all of you will, too.

Larry Parrish
October 17, 2017
Fort Gaines, Georgia

Introduction

From 1969 to 2004, the Montreal Expos were a mainstay in Major League Baseball, although barely, at the end, before their departure to Washington, DC.

Montreal has been too long without a Major League Baseball club.

During the strike-shortened 1981 season, the Expos captured the hearts of Canadian baseball fans by making the playoffs for the only time in franchise history. Even though the Toronto Blue Jays were in the midst of their fifth season, they didn't yet enjoy the lofty status in Canada that the Expos had.

The Expos played 10 playoff games that October, only to be rocked on Blue Monday, the 19th, late in the afternoon, by a player named Monday. Rick Monday.

That depressing day for Montreal fans, executives, and players has left an indelible mark on the city's baseball history. That's why it's called Blue Monday.

Typically, any Monday may be "blue." The first day of work after a weekend off for most people around the world, Monday can be depressing. Monday blues, some people call it.

Historically, people believe that the bluest Mondays typically take place in January, which is one of the bleakest months of the year because in this hemisphere winter has taken its hard grip. But Expos followers have a special reason to get discouraged by "I Don't Like Mondays" by the British band the Boomtown Rats. "Monday, Monday" by the Mamas & the Papas must be equally maddening. Then there's "Manic Monday," written by Prince and recorded by the Bangles, about a girl not wanting to go to work on Monday and preferring Sunday, her "I don't-have-to-run-day."

This book endeavours to pay tribute to the 1981 Expos and the 1981 Los Angeles Dodgers, who won the World Series that year. The book is intended to give scope, depth, exposure, and added recognition to Rick Monday, not only for what he did that day but outside that day. He was a man of service in the U.S. Marine Corps Reserve. He was a star at Arizona State University and the first pick in the first-ever draft of amateur players in June 1965. He rescued a Stars and Stripes flag from demonstrators who were about to torch it during a game in 1976. He enjoyed a solid career of 19 seasons in the big leagues.

Equally, the book pays tribute to Steve Rogers, who coughed up the home run to Monday. He has graciously faced the music ever since. It's been a burden on him in some ways but it doesn't appear to have bothered him *too* much.

What the Expos did in 1981 was awkward but rewarding. Thanks in part to Wallace Johnson's historic triple, they slipped into the playoffs October 3 on the basis of winning the second half of the National League East following a lengthy strike. They beat the Philadelphia Phillies 3–2 in a best-of-five set some called a National League mini-series. Officially, it was one of two National League Division Series that year, the Expos against the Phillies in one, with the Los Angeles Dodgers and Houston Astros playing the other.

This book had me reaching out to interview 73 people. What transpired were many stories, tales, and yarns I had never heard before. A lot of beans were spilled. Secrets were unlocked and old narratives examined.

I delve into the discovery of Tim Raines of Sanford, Florida, by the Expos' Canadian-born scout Bill MacKenzie; Ellis Valentine's demise as a flawed individual; and Dick Williams's firing and Jim Fanning's hiring a few weeks prior to the playoffs. Blue Monday itself resulted in close to 12 intertwining chapters here, many centring on Monday.

I would think that this book might have the impetus to be optioned someday for a movie. In the meantime, enjoy.

Part One

THE LONG
LEAD-IN

Chapter 1

Expos Sign Williams,
Pursue Jackson

When the rubble of the Expos' disastrous 1976 season had settled, team president John McHale and sidekick Jim Fanning didn't look that far in searching for a new manager. Career minor-league manager Karl Kuehl had been a disaster in 1976, and McHale said it was a mistake to have fired Gene Mauch, who managed the team from 1969 through 1975.

So where did the Expos cast their eyes? To a former Toronto Triple-A Maple Leafs skipper, who had been manager of the Boston Red Sox in 1967 to 1969, of the Oakland A's that won three consecutive championships from 1972 to 1974, and then of the California Angels in 1975 and '76.

Dick Williams was considered a turnaround maestro. He guided the Maple Leafs to two consecutive International League titles in 1965 and 1966 and took the Red Sox "Impossible Dream" team led by Carl Yastrzemski to the 1967 World Series before they lost to the St. Louis Cardinals. He had spunk and didn't care if he ruffled a player's feelings.

Fanning and McHale were familiar with Williams because he had been the Expos' third-base coach under Mauch in 1970, a brief respite for Williams after he was let go by the Red Sox following the 1969 season. When

Angels manager Dick Williams's feisty attitude with umpires was what the Expos wanted.

he joined the Expos in 1970, Williams had sat back and retooled his thinking strategies while watching the tactician Mauch — that is, when he wasn't hitting fungoes before games or flashing signals to runners and batters during them. The Montreal job gave him a different perspective on managing.

So when Williams left the Angels after his stint with them ended in 1976, Williams called the Expos and asked that he be given the job. He didn't wait for the Expos to approach him. That's how aggressive he was. He felt confident that he would be hired, and he was.

Williams was given a five-year contract. Hiring Williams was the beginning of the rejuvenation of the Expos after a 55–107 season in 1976.

"Dick was a known manager. He was feisty and we weren't a feisty club," ex-team owner Charles Bronfman said in 2017.

McHale figured Williams would light a fire under his charges much like he did with the Boston, Oakland, and California squads, which were known to have a few players who would fight on occasion with each other or almost come to blows with Williams himself.

Angels manager Dick Williams, right, chats with outfielder Frank Robinson in this photo taken in 1974. Both would go on to be Expos managers, Williams from 1977 to 1981, Robinson from 2002 to 2004.

The attempted remodelling of the Expos didn't stop with Williams. McHale went so far as to try to entice superstar free agent Reggie Jackson to come to Montreal. Jackson had been one of Williams's players in Oakland and the two helped steer the A's to glory. Jackson had spent the 1976 season with the Baltimore Orioles, a brief stopover during his splendid career.

"Reggie was available," former Expos secretary-treasurer Harry Renaud recalled. "He was such a superstar. We flew him into Montreal. We organized a reception for him — the whole weekend. We met with the media, the pooh-bahs, including the mayor, Jean Drapeau.

"Reggie was late. He came down to the stadium and arrived with an entourage; a bunch of them came in a trailer. There were all these hangers-on. It was a travel party. I couldn't figure that out. They were all smoking dope. It was kind of strange with his stature. We had such a big party at Charles's place. There were about 50 people involved.

"The party ended on a Saturday night," Renaud said. "Reggie departed very suddenly. Next thing, he just up and left. There were no goodbyes. That was the end of the story."

The next night, Jackson and Bronfman's close friend Leo Kolber, a member of the team's board of directors, tried to hammer out a deal. McHale and Kolber offered Jackson a five-year deal for just under $5 million.

Apparently, Jackson came to the meeting looking and feeling like death warmed over. "Reggie had a terrible hangover," Kolber said. "He needed a hair of the dog."

Rather than seeking another alcoholic drink, Jackson looked at Kolber's son Jonathan and said, "Hey, kid, make me a milkshake, but it has to have eggs in it."

Jackson also met with the media while he was in Montreal and said he was very interested in the Expos, especially since he knew Williams from their days in Oakland. Williams even took Jackson on a tour of Olympic Stadium as it was being prepped for the Expos' first season there in 1977.

"I want to know if these gentlemen want to build a contender. There's a lot more than signing for a lot of money," Jackson told the reporters surrounding him. "If Dick Williams hadn't been here, I wouldn't be here. People tell me that you have the most beautiful girls in the world here."

The enthusiasm both sides showed prompted Bronfman to tell the media, "I think we are pretty much in agreement on fundamentals."

As one of the game's biggest stars, Jackson was also drawing a lot of interest at that time from the Yankees, Baltimore Orioles, and San Diego Padres.

Ultimately, Jackson accepted a much less lucrative deal with the Yankees: five years for about $3 million plus a Rolls-Royce.

As Renaud said, there are different versions as to why Jackson spurned the Expos. "It had something to do with crossing the border. He was held up by customs at the border. Apparently, he had an unregistered gun. Phone calls were made to Marc Lalonde, the minister of justice, and Reggie was allowed into the country," Renaud added.

One report suggested that he was held up at the airport in Ottawa, not at Montreal's Dorval Airport, because some marijuana was found in his clothes. Another report said Jackson was simply upset that customs people were rummaging through his clothes, period. McHale had told reporters that he and other team officials discussed Jackson's drug case and came away satisfied that he was "not a historical user of drugs" and that he had talked things over with the police. No charges were laid.

"We are absolutely convinced he has no drug problem," Bronfman weighed in at the time.

"I thought we had a good chance with Reggie. They negotiated at Leo's place. Reggie left … there's an old baseball saying, 'If he leaves without signing, he's gone,'" Bronfman noted, 41 years later. "Reggie made the right decision, no question. George Steinbrenner said one time, 'Ray Kroc of the Padres might have McDonald's, Bronfman might have Seagram's, but I have the Big Apple.'"

Jackson and the Yankees proceeded to win the World Series in both of his first two seasons in New York, both series being against the Dodgers.

Years earlier, on New Year's Eve in 1974, Renaud and McHale had tried to lure another free-agent stud to the Expos: Catfish Hunter. The Expos duo had flown down on Bronfman's Seagram jet to get to Hunter's hometown of Hertford, North Carolina. "It's a great story," Renaud said. "It was eight in the morning and there we were in this old small town. There was this country-type lawyer, and he said, 'Would you like a Coke?' There was no coffee. Then Catfish came in and joined the meeting. What I remember [being] funny about it was that Catfish came in with a Styrofoam cup and was chewing tobacco and spitting in the cup.

"We came out of the meeting very high. We made a great presentation. So we got back to Montreal and we were dressed to go to a New Year's party and we heard the radio flash that he had signed with the Yankees."

Give Bronfman and the Expos credit. They made huge efforts to sign people like Jackson and Hunter, but failed.

Chapter 2

The Discovery of Tim Raines

The Expos' spring-training hub in 1977 was in the north-central Florida tourist town of Daytona Beach. As the team was going through the paces that spring, they were tipped off about a high-school player who was suiting up for a game in the same town. The young man was a must-see prospect, and he turned out to be a diamond in the rough.

It came about as the team's Canadian-born scouting assistant Bill MacKenzie was hanging around the office at the Expos' City Island Ballpark facility, getting ready for another day.

"During spring training, a number of us in the office would talk in the morning, take calls, check on scouts to see what coverage they were doing and stuff like that," MacKenzie related. "In the afternoon, I would put on my uniform and go out and coach. One morning, I got a phone call. I picked up. I don't know why I did. I guess the secretary must have had a late night or something. There was this lady on the phone. She said, 'Does your organization know anything about this kid out of Seminole High School in Sanford, Florida, by the name of Tim Raines? He's playing about 3:30 today at Daytona High School. You might want to take a look at him.'

"It was an anonymous caller. To this day, I don't know who it was. I don't know if it was Tim's mother or someone else."

While keeping the woman on the phone, MacKenzie checked the team's files and got back on the line. "I have access to everything here, but no, we have nothing on him," MacKenzie told the caller.

MacKenzie decided he was going to check out Raines. "I just said I had this call about this little black guy from Seminole High School. So I went to the high school and watched him take practice and stuff like that. Here was Raines, a five-foot-eight shortstop for the Seminole Seminoles. He was a skinny little fart about 135 pounds. I said, 'Ooh, he can't play shortstop.' He had no range.

"But anything he hit — and he was only a right-handed hitter then — was to right-centre. He didn't turn on the ball. He hit a ball to right-centre in the gap and you swore you saw Willie Mays running. It was really exciting, watching him run. You could see that he would be a good player. He had that athleticism. *There's an athlete*, I thought as I looked at him. From that time on, we had Raines on our radar.

"He was the best athlete Seminole had, and they had to play him at shortstop. I said, 'Tim, if you have a shot at going anywhere, you are going to have to do it as a second-baseman or outfielder. I understand the situation here. You have to play shortstop on this team because you're the best player they've got.' Absolutely, I told him that. He thanked me for suggesting that he should move."

MacKenzie knew how to read talent. He was born in Pictou, Nova Scotia, but spent most of his youth in Sarnia, Ontario. Like many Canadian kids, MacKenzie loved to play baseball, and along the way he found himself at St. Clair County Community College in Port Huron, Michigan, near Sarnia, where he was given a lot of look-sees by the Detroit Tigers' bird-dog scout Harry Moore, who kept recommending that the Tigers sign the catching prospect.

MacKenzie finally did sign, in 1966. He played in the minors for both the Tigers and Expos before his playing career was abruptly ended when he banged up his left shoulder in a home-plate collision. Following the 1972 season, which he spent with the Tigers in a non-playing role, MacKenzie got work with the Expos as a scouting assistant.

With all of his experience, MacKenzie had a knack for spotting a prospect like Raines. MacKenzie proudly tells people that he was the first member of the Expos' scouting staff to witness Raines in action. "Funny thing is, Bill Adair, our Florida area scout, didn't like Raines," MacKenzie said, shaking his head.

That's right, Adair didn't see anything in Raines. Adair was a career minor-league manager, including a number of stints in the Expos' farm system, and he was the bullpen coach for the major-league team under Karl Kuehl in 1976.

"Bill didn't want to draft Raines because he thought he wasn't a prospect. Bill wrote him off," MacKenzie said.

"I said, 'Bill, he's an athlete.' He was like Willie Mays running the bases. He knew when to take the extra base. He wasn't a Punch-and-Judy hitter. When he hit a gapper, it was so exciting to see him run. He was such a beautiful young man. So we told Bill that if he didn't want to draft him that we would draft him right out of the front office. So that's what we did. We drafted him out of the front office. It was Bill who actually got him to sign the contract, but he wasn't the one who did the spade work. I did."

Too often, a scouting director gets more credit than the actual scout who makes the initial discovery, the finding of the player, the following of the player and recommending him. In the Expos' media guides of subsequent years, Raines's bio said, "Signed by Bill Adair." But that's misleading, because Adair had no input in signing him.

"When the day of the draft came up in June 1977, we were hoping Tim's name wouldn't come up and be called by another team. We were sweating bullets," MacKenzie said.

Sitting in a war room at the Americana Hotel on West 38th Street in midtown Manhattan, the Expos, under scouting director Danny Menendez, plucked Raines in the fifth round. Earlier in that draft, the Expos had taken pitcher Bill Gullickson as their first choice. Then they took pitchers Gregory Staffron, Scott Sanderson, and Scott Anderson before picking Raines. Gullickson, Sanderson, and Raines all made the majors out of that 1977 draft.

"So we put Raines in our instructional league," MacKenzie said. "What he did that 1977–78 off-season was put on about 40 pounds and he learned how to be a switch-hitter. He learned how to hit left. It ended up he hit better left-handed than right-handed."

Raines's Seminole baseball coach Bobby Lundquist remembers a fun-loving, joking, humble athlete in Raines. Lundquist said Raines excelled in football, baseball, track and field, and basketball at Seminole.

"Tim was a tremendous running back. He didn't have world-class speed but he had unbelievable balance," Lundquist recalled. "Nobody could tackle him. He'd get 10 yards a carry. Everybody stood up when he had the ball. He was a gifted natural athlete."

One of Lundquist's regrets is that he didn't get Raines to learn how to switch-hit in high school, and he admits that Raines played out of position at shortstop because he was the team's best athlete. MacKenzie was right.

In his book *Rock Solid*, released in 2017, Raines wrote that the Dodgers spent considerable time sizing him up at Sanford Memorial Stadium and other high schools, but they never did draft him.

"I wish I could remember the scout from the Dodgers coming out to the park to show Tim how to turn a double play and to get out of the way without getting hit because your legs are valuable," Lundquist said.

In fact, many major-league teams took a look at Raines, according to Lundquist. Specifically, Lundquist mentioned Andy Seminick of the Phillies and George Zuraw of the Reds.

"I do remember the Expos coming out and showing interest," Lundquist said. "The knock on Tim in high school was that he had no set place to play in the infield or outfield. He wasn't a good shortstop. No question he had the athleticism, the speed, but he didn't have the size," Lundquist added. "He didn't look like 'that stud.' But he proved everyone wrong."

In basketball, if the team needed a last-second shot to win the game, Raines was the player. Even in baseball, Raines wasn't just an infielder and hitter; he could pitch, too. He could come in late in the game and get the last three outs. Lundquist recalls distinctly that Raines hit much better in his junior year than in his senior year.

Lundquist chuckles when he relates the story of how someone at Seminole came up to him and said the hurdles team needed "points" at a county meet so Raines stepped up and won the 330-yard hurdles in a time of what Lundquist remembers as 33 seconds, a record they say has never been broken in that part of Florida.

It was very classy of Raines to mention Lundquist in his book *Rock Solid*. All too often lesser lights such as high-school coaches don't get enough credit from pro athletes.

"You know, I will tell you this, that nothing Tim did surprised me," Lundquist said. "He was that kind of athlete. I wasn't surprised with his longevity and success. He was always very humble. He never allowed his success to become bigger than the moment. He was very likeable as a person. He had a big, infectious smile.

"Tim always beat whoever he was facing. It was a testament to the competitiveness and the humbleness he kept."

Raines's father, Ned Sr., had played semi-pro baseball in Florida. Siblings Ned and Levi were no slouches either. His other brothers were Tommy and Samuel and he also had a sister, Patricia. Sadly, another sister, Anita Gail, died in 1968 when she was only four years old after being hit by a vehicle near the family home.

"Levi was the best athlete in the Raines family," Lundquist said. "Ned, he was a little smaller and stockier than Tim, but Ned could hit the ball. When he hit the ball, there was an unmistaken sound. He hit it so hard, it was scary."

It was somewhat symbolic that Raines was born and grew up in the town where Jackie Robinson once lived. But the situation had definitely changed since the 1940s, when black ball players were less accepted by society. There was a day in 1946, for example, during spring training, when the police chief in Sanford actually threatened to stop a game if Robinson did not leave the field. Robinson complied.

Like their hard-working father, who was employed by Hubbard Construction as a grader operator, the Raines sons (other than Tim) plied their lifetime trades in construction. Mother Florence was a school custodian and Patricia also worked in the school system.

"Tim and I were a year apart. He was a year older," Ned Jr. told me. "He always batted in front of me. I would hit cleanup. Tim and I did a lot of playing sports together — football, basketball, baseball."

Tim's mother, Florence (Sue), mentioned how Tim and his brothers would play baseball on a dirt road called Bungalow Boulevard, and told a funny story about how they loved using an unusual household item to play — an item that was around the same size and shape as a baseball.

"Tim would always take the top off my dishwasher and use it as a ball," the matriarch told me.

"I remember Ned and I slinging that thing around," Tim said, laughing.

"That dish top was the best baseball we had," Ned Jr. said. "We'd throw curveballs, breaking balls with it. We played with that thing until we quit playing, until it got too dark to play ball. That's how we learned. We got better by playing against each other."

As his sister Patricia recollects, "Tim had no problems with his lessons, but he was more into sports. Tim and I were pretty close. He was younger than me. We played a lot together. I had to go to some of the baseball games. They were long, long, long. I remember teaching him how to drive a car. I was 17 or so."

Raines was the only black regular on the Seminole team, although there were others who were backups. Same with his Pony League team. He was the only black player on the roster.

"I kept talking to him," his mother told me. "I told him, 'If you want to make it, you can't stay out all night.' Every team, everybody he played against beat him on the field, but he hung in there."

"Tim is one of my best friends," said ex-Seminole teammate Don Williams, who has been Raines's lawyer for the past 20 years. Williams remembers another player who was almost as good as Raines in both football and baseball: Wayne Tolleson.

"We kept hearing Tolly this, Tolly that," Williams said. "I told somebody …, 'Write this down. Tim will be in the Hall of Fame one day.' I meant it. He stood out so much. He was phenomenal back then, not just in baseball, but [at] football and track and field. Some 50 colleges tried to recruit him."

Sanford sure loves one of its own: Tim Raines.

Chapter 3

The 1977 and 1978 Seasons

Mel Didier was gone by the time the 1977 Expos' season had begun, but you could say it was his team. His stamp was all over it, and he had helped to lay the groundwork for the great Expos teams of 1979, 1980, and 1981.

This was a team ready to make its mark in baseball. It took time, but the ingredients and seeds were there, and Didier, the director of scouting and player development, had planted them. He had received tremendous support from owner Charles Bronfman and top executives John McHale and Jim Fanning.

Didier, who died in 2017 at age 90, was a protegé of Expos general manager John McHale, just as Jim Fanning had been. All three had worked together in the Milwaukee Braves organization. It was McHale who coaxed Didier into joining the Expos in the fall of 1968, luring him away from his job as running backs/freshmen coach at Didier's alma mater, Louisiana State University.

"Mel built the Expos as far as I'm concerned," said Larry Parrish, a third-baseman out of Winter Haven, Florida, who was an undrafted free agent until Didier came along and signed him in 1972. There were 13 other teams lined up in earnest, wanting Parrish to sign with them, but it was Didier who most impressed Parrish's father, Alton.

"Mel, Red Smith, and Zack Taylor all had a hand in signing me," Parrish said. "Red was the area scout and Zack was the east-coast cross-checker, but Mel came to the house and talked money. I was offered more money by the Orioles, but my dad was sold on Mel and what he stood for.

"I was a unique case. I wasn't drafted out of high school. I went to junior college and led the nation in hitting, so before the draft I was a free agent and could sign with anyone. I don't remember the details of bonus offers anymore, but they were nothing compared to what these guys get today, but new cars then cost about $4,000." (That was a hint that Parrish got himself a free car out of the Expos.)

Also under Didier's watch, prodigious talents Gary Carter, Andre Dawson, Warren Cromartie, Ellis Valentine, and Steve Rogers were drafted and signed. However, one draft pick did get away: Condredge Holloway, a hotshot athlete from Lee High School in Huntsville, Alabama, who was a mighty fine athlete in a baseball uniform along with being a standout on the gridiron. Didier took Holloway as the Expos' Number-1 selection in 1971 and then followed up in that year's secondary draft phase by picking Rogers first.

"We lost a Number-1 pick in Holloway but we got Rogers in the secondary draft," said long-time Expos scouting assistant and broadcaster Rodger Brulotte. "Holloway would have been a starting shortstop for us. He didn't sign with us because his mother wanted him to get an education, so he went to the University of Tennessee. We know what he did in football with Toronto and Ottawa in the Canadian Football League, but he was a heckuva shortstop."

Not all of Didier's draftees were star players, but productive part-time players such as Jerry White showed up on Didier's radar. He saw an athlete in White and took the young player out of San Francisco's Washington High School in 1970. White would turn out to be a pretty decent player as a fourth outfielder and became a fashion impresario after he got lessons from early-franchise manager and cosmopolitan man-about-town Gene Mauch.

"Mel was just like another dad to me. He and Jim Fanning took care of me," White said. "Mel was always a strong personality. When he came

This unique photo gathers many of the great young minds, coaches, scouts, and administrators of the Expos in the 1970s. Left to right are future 1981 Expos hitting coach Pat Mullin, Jack Damaska, Lance Nichols, Walt Hriniak, Bill MacKenzie, Bill Adair, Mel Didier, Karl Kuehl, Bobby Mattick, Larry Bearnarth, and Rodger Brulotte. Didier was the architect of the Expos, with many players from his era still playing for Montreal in the 1980s.

around, he said that as long as you were doing things right, there was nothing to worry about. He brought out a whip. He was tough. Whether you were a first-round pick or the 50th, he treated everyone the same."

Didier was a disciplinarian of sorts, a manager who wasn't averse to running warm-ups like football practices. He also demanded complete loyalty to the organization through fashion.

"Mel said you could wear no other logos except the Expos logo, and that meant caps, sweaters, anything," Brulotte said. "After that, I never wore another logo except the Expos logo. I'll never ever forget three people for allowing Mel the leeway to do what he wanted to do. They never questioned him. They were Charles Bronfman, John McHale, and Jim Fanning."

Said Bronfman, "Mel Didier was a man who was cut in the mould of John McHale. He was every inch a gentleman and gave everything he had in building the minor-league system for us. I can't speak highly enough of him."

The 1977 season turned out to be a lot better than the disaster of 1976. Under the tutelage of first-year manager Dick Williams and his coaching staff of Jim Brewer, Billy Gardner, Mickey Vernon, and Ozzie Virgil Sr., the Expos improved to 75–87 from 55–107.

It was the first full season for Dawson and Valentine. Already in the fold were Steve Rogers, Warren Cromartie, and Larry Parrish. Infused with organizational players were veterans obtained from other teams in trades, among them Dave Cash, Tim Foli, Mike Jorgensen, Tony Pérez, and Chris Speier.

One of the surprises that year was Canadian-born pitcher Bill Atkinson of Chatham, Ontario, who spent the entire season with the Expos, crafting a neat 7–2 record and 3.35 ERA in 83.1 innings, all in relief. And he did it despite his small stature, making believers out of the doubters. Not before and not after that season did he spin that magic that he spun in 1977.

"The highlight for me personally that year was playing the whole season in the big leagues," Atkinson said. "I was five foot eight, 155 pounds. A lot of people with more talent wished they could have done what I did. It was just one of those things. I went to spring training that year and I got called up. Everything worked out for me. What more can I say?

"A year or two earlier, I had gone to winter ball in Mexico and the manager was this guy Clint Courtney. And he said to me, 'They sent me a little shit like you?' I said, 'I guess I'm the little guy.'"

Coming from Courtney, that comment seemed odd. Atkinson couldn't remember if Courtney was serious or was joking, but Courtney was a mere five foot eight himself. Imagine him calling Atkinson a "little shit." Courtney had managed to hang around the majors for 11 seasons, first as a catcher and later as a manager in the Braves' farm system when he wasn't managing winter-ball teams. But Atkinson sure made Courtney a believer. "I ended up going 5–1 that winter with an ERA of 0.68," Atkinson told me.

When the 1978 season rolled around, Atkinson was back and determined to show that he belonged. Unfortunately, it didn't quite work out that way, and the Expos as a whole took a little step back. On the plus side, their record actually improved slightly, to 76–86. And there were some other positive aspects to the season: Ross Grimsley became the first and only pitcher in Expos history to win 20 games, when he went 20–11; shortstop Chris Speier hit for the cycle on July 20; and the team pounded out 28 hits in shellacking the Atlanta Braves 19–0 on July 30.

"I was a free agent and signed with Montreal. It was a young team with a great future," Grimsley recalled. "It had the nucleus of a really outstanding team. I was looking forward to the weather; I really liked the cold weather. The contract was a big thing. It helped make the decision easier. I got a six-year contract, which was a little uncommon.

"It was probably one of the best years that I had pitching-wise and concentration-wise. I loved the stadium, I loved the weather. What stood out was that I was just so locked in. I didn't throw really hard. I was a control-type guy. I won my 20th game in the last game of the season. My whole family was there in St. Louis. My family got to see it."

Chapter 4

Coming So Close:
1979 and 1980

The 1979 and 1980 editions of the Expos were two of the most talented teams in franchise history, but both ultimately fell short.

In 1979, the Expos came close, only to lose out to the Pittsburgh Pirates. The team boasted a record of 95–65, finishing just two games behind the Pirates. It was heartbreaking for the Expos to win so many games and not win the division.

In 1980, the Expos came close again, only to lose out to another Pennsylvania team, the Phillies, this time by only one game.

"We were starting to develop and we had a special belief that we had a strong chance to win," star catcher Gary Carter said about the 1979 season. Alas, the Expos had to play a significant part of the end of that season without Carter after he sustained a hand injury.

Not even a trade to reacquire early-franchise hero Rusty Staub from the Detroit Tigers helped much. He arrived July 19, but ended up batting a disappointing .267 over 38 games. He didn't actually get much playing time, because Tony Pérez was rock-solid at first and the outfield was manned by the capable trio of Andre Dawson, Ellis Valentine, and Warren Cromartie. Also, with the Expos being in the National League, Staub could not be a designated hitter.

On July 27, however, Staub played his first home game following the trade and it was memorable. A crowd of 59,260 jammed the Big O to welcome him home. It was a doubleheader against the Pirates and Staub didn't play in the first game. But in the nightcap, when he came in as a pinch-hitter at 8:36 p.m., there was deafening roar after deafening roar, prompting him to doff his cap more than once in appreciation and causing a delay in the game. Staub attempted to step into the batter's box several times but was forced to step out as the fans roared their approval again. Staub doffed his cap. When Grant Jackson finally got to pitch to Staub, the fan favourite flied out. "That's the only time the crowds affected me as much during an at-bat in my career," Staub said later.

That outfield trio of Cromartie, Dawson, and Valentine compared mightily with the 1994 combo of Moises Alou, Larry Walker, and Marquis Grissom, except, Cromartie said, "How do you compare? They had it all, too. They probably covered more ground. We were all fundamentally sound. Mel Didier groomed all of us."

The Expos had really begun to gel as a franchise after years of being doormats. The farm system and scouting department had finally started producing some exceptional home-grown talent.

"All these players were developed properly in the minor leagues," said Jim Fanning, who became the Expos' farm director in the late 1970s after years as the team's GM. "They advanced to the big leagues and stayed. In some cases, earlier on, players advanced and fell back. We had really good minor-league managers in Doc Edwards and Felipe Alou, who was a great teacher in our development program."

Near the end of the 1979 season, the Pirates and Expos met in Montreal for a three-game series. Willie Stargell came to the plate September 19 to face right-hander Dale Murray, who had been acquired in August from the Mets. Stargell connected and the ball went into the right-field seats, giving the Bucs a win and a two-game lead in the NL East, a cushion they would never relinquish. The Expos finished at 95–65, the Pirates at 98–67.

"In 1979, we had no relievers and that cost us," said long-time Expos scouting assistant and broadcaster Rodger Brulotte.

"We back-doored the pennant in 1979," Cromartie recalled. "The biggest memories for me were of how young we were and the great manager we had in Dick Williams. I never thought in my wildest dreams that he'd be my manager.

"Dick was perfect for us. He meant the world to me. He gave me the chance to play every day. It was pretty huge. He gave Rodney Scott a chance to play. He loved Rodney. Dick deserves a lot of credit. We were making a name for ourselves. We were fundamentally sound. We were happy to be playing at the Big O."

Yes, Rodney Scott was something else. Playing full-time, he had three homers, 42 RBI, and 39 stolen bases. He stole third base at will, usually when the catcher was throwing the ball back to the pitcher.

"Rodney Scott was unbelievable, so exciting," Brulotte said.

"That was the first year the Expos played over .500," remembered Russ Hansen, a long-time Expos fan and photographer who shot hundreds of pictures over the years and shared many of them with Expos players and personnel. "That year, I saved every newspaper article from the *Montreal Star, Montreal Gazette, Sunday Express,* and so on and put everything in a scrapbook. It's about five inches thick. I want to take all of that information and write a book. In 1995, I lent the scrapbook to [former Expos right-fielder] Ellis Valentine. I'm still trying to get it back from him. He says it's up in his attic somewhere."

Through their first 10 seasons, the Expos had played below .500, so this was some sweet turnaround. After two consecutive losing seasons under Williams, the Expos had finally turned heads with that 95-win season.

"Nineteen seventy-nine was the first year we really matured and turned the corner. We felt we could compete with anybody," Larry Parrish said. "You know, we had one of those great pennant races with the Pirates. We won something like 24 games in the month of September and didn't gain any ground on the Pirates. We played great that year. At the all-star break, Willie Stargell of the Pirates was having a so-so year. He was getting toward the end of his career and people thought he was done." Parrish laughed. "Unfortunately, in the second half, the weather warmed up, and so did Willie. We played great and the Pirates played super also."

Remarkably, Stargell, at age 39, would be voted the National League's Most Valuable Player, the NLCS MVP, and the World Series MVP that year. It was the first time a player had copped all three awards. And he did it, leading the "We Are Family" Pirates to the World Series.

At spring training in 1980, Rusty Staub was having contract problems with the Expos. He also had a fight on his hands, with Warren Cromartie also vying for the first-base job after Tony Pérez left as a free agent. In late March, Staub was traded and Cromartie officially came in from the outfield to take over first.

"I loved first base," Cromartie said. "It was my favourite position. I started at first in Little League. Left field was a very difficult position. It was a learning position. I didn't throw that good. They were running on me. The press was trying to say Rusty was traded because of me and that there was a rivalry between us. Rusty and I always laughed at that. Rusty is a very, very good friend of mine. In 1980, I played all 162 games."

That year, the Expos went down to the wire again, meeting the Phillies in a three-game series in Montreal. "The 1980 final season weekend was my beginning," Phillies third-baseman Mike Schmidt told me years ago. "I'll never forget hitting home runs to win the first two games of the series against Montreal in which we had to win two out of three. The clincher came in the 11th inning of the final game of the season with first base open and Don Montgomery on deck — a call-up kid, who had never batted in the major leagues."

Setting the stage for this drama was Phillies catcher Bob Boone, who doubled into the left-centre gap. There were two out and first base was open. Coming to the plate was none other than Schmidt. Instead of putting him on, Williams elected to allow reliever Stan Bahnsen to pitch to Schmidt because Bahnsen had enjoyed pretty good success against Schmidt during the regular season.

"Stan Bahnsen owned me that year, but he took me too lightly," Schmidt remembered of that at-bat. "After throwing two sliders for balls, he left a fastball out over the plate, and the rest is history. I'll never forget that moment."

Said Fanning, "Schmidt hit a giant home run. He was an outstanding hitter and you expect that from outstanding hitters."

What does Cromartie remember about that home run? "What do you mean?" he replied. "From 1979 to 1983, we didn't get lucky. Whether it was a pinch hit, a home run here, a home run there, the wrong pitcher … it wasn't meant to be."

"The 1979, 1980 teams were better than 1981," said Alain Usereau, who authored the fascinating book *The Expos in Their Prime*. "There was more depth on the teams in '79 and '80. The pitching staffs in 1979 and '80 were underrated because the focus was on these young players — Dawson, Carter, Valentine, Cromartie, Parrish.

"The pitching staff in 1994 might have been the best in the team's history. There was no weak arm. Butch Henry was one of the best lefties in the game for two years. I admit I have a bias toward the teams of my teenage years (1979–80).

"But looking at 1994 with a cool head, I must admit they had quite a team, but probably not as deep organization-wise as those of the late 1970s. They had a bunch of injuries in 1980 and they still managed to compete. I really doubt they would have been able to overcome that, had it happened in 1994."

After coming oh-so-close in 1979 and 1980, the Expos were looking to take the next step in 1981.

Part Two

1981: THE YEAR THAT WAS

Chapter 5

Is This the Year?

When Expos spring training rolled around in 1981, it was at a site already familiar to some: Municipal Stadium in West Palm Beach.

From 1969 through 1971, the Expos had trained at this very ballpark before transferring operations to City Island in Daytona Beach from 1972 to 1980.

"For one thing, we were getting back to a better stadium," Expos owner Charles Bronfman recalled about the switch back.

"Daytona was supposed to be a temporary fix, but we were there for years," Expos secretary-treasurer Harry Renaud said. "We were second cousins in Daytona. West Palm Beach was much better from every standpoint. We just weren't comfortable in Daytona. We had to do more travelling for spring-training games."

The move back to West Palm Beach was a big loss for the fans in Daytona Beach, but it would be a boon for general manager John McHale and Expos players who lived in the area. Over time, a number of players, such as Jeff Reardon, Tommy Hutton, Bill Gullickson, and Gary Carter, along with announcer Dave Van Horne, would purchase properties there, especially in Palm Beach Gardens, near the PGA National golf course.

But something more noteworthy than the change of location really rattled the Expos during spring training that year. On March 20, commissioner Bowie Kuhn made a decision that would have grave repercussions on the franchise's status across Canada. The decision was to cut into the Expos' television rights from coast to coast, which would reduce the team's exposure. The Toronto Blue Jays had joined the American League in 1977 and had complained about the Expos cutting into their coverage area in Ontario, so Kuhn did something about it.

"I was really, really upset," Bronfman said in 2017. "I told him he had a big problem. I told him I had gotten into baseball as a unifying thing for the country. I told him. 'Goddamn it, this television deal jeopardizes the Expos. It's going to break up Canada.' He said there was not much he could do about it."

As Renaud recalled, the Kuhn decision meant the Expos games could not be broadcast into the Toronto area; nor could they do any broadcasting into the Golden Horseshoe area west of Toronto.

"We felt the Expos were Canada's national team, and therefore should have rights to the entire country," Renaud said. "Kuhn came in and said the Expos had the French market, which was Quebec, but that there would be limits in Toronto and the Golden Horseshoe. It screwed up our market. The decision should have involved two leagues, but his decision went beyond the scope of the league presidents."

Bronfman would later ask succeeding commissioner Peter Ueberroth to review Kuhn's decision, but he didn't get very far. "Ueberroth got back to me and said we could get more games in Ontario but that we would pay more money," Bronfman said. "I started to laugh and he said, 'What's funny?' And I said he called my bluff, he called my hand. To cross Toronto's territory, we had to cough up more money."

But back to spring training. This was a chance for rookies like Tim Raines and Tim Wallach to really shine. With speedster Ron LeFlore gone after having a falling-out with manager Dick Williams and GM John McHale, Raines would try to step in to replace him.

Wallach had been drafted out of Cal State-Fullerton as a first-baseman, but he was earmarked for the outfield with the Expos before eventually becoming an all-star third-baseman. But in 1981, as a part-time player, he would be happy just to contribute anywhere.

Wallach enjoyed a superlative spring that year, after turning heads with his 1980 season in Triple-A with Denver, but he had to earn a spot in the Expos lineup. It wasn't a case of the Expos keeping him for the sake of keeping him: he was so stellar that beat writers voted him top rookie during the Grapefruit League schedule in March. Wallach opened a lot of eyes — in spring training the year before, the writers hadn't noticed any rookies who particularly stood out so they hadn't even bothered to select one. "I had a good spring. I hit something like five home runs," Wallach recalled.

"Wallach hit for good average in college and in the minors and had big-time home run numbers. He lived with the power bat. He was a smart player," recalled Bob Gebhard, who was the Expos' farm director at the time and saw Wallach play numerous times in the minor leagues.

Aside from looking at in-house prospects and a slew of veterans already on the team, McHale was on the lookout to improve the club through the trade route. He had fine-tuned the roster a little in the fall of 1980 by signing free-agent outfielder Willie Montanez to a two-year deal worth $600,000 and re-upped with reliever Stan Bahnsen for three years for a total of a million bucks. Considering that was 1981, an average annual stipend of $333,000 was a pretty good piece of change for Bahnsen.

As spring training wore on, McHale had tried to trade closer Neil Allen away from the Mets for talented but troublesome outfielder Ellis Valentine. The Mets said no.

Other teams wanted Raines, but McHale wasn't giving him up under any circumstances. Same with Wallach. There was also the unsettling news going around baseball that the Expos were listening to offers for star pitcher Steve Rogers. Rogers wanted the canard addressed once and for all and approached McHale. He was told nothing was in the works.

What didn't get a lot of attention was the five-year contract outfielder Andre Dawson signed for something like $6 million. Looking at that contract with a fine-tooth comb was catcher Gary Carter, who was seeking a deal that would pay him $2 million per year. I remember, as a freelance writer for Toronto's *Globe and Mail*, travelling to my native Renfrew, Ontario, from Toronto to meet Carter for the first time. He was there attending a sports banquet in January 1981. The obvious topic of conversation between us was the contract situation. He said he wanted a contract extension.

Not long into the season, a rare occurrence prompted the baseball world to stand up and take notice of the Expos. When Enos Cabell of the Giants flied out to deep centre on the night of May 10, 1981, Expos pitcher Charlie Lea had accomplished what few in Major League Baseball have done: he threw a no-hitter to lead the Expos past San Francisco 4–0 at Olympic Stadium.

"I tired in the eighth inning because that's the longest I've gone all season," Lea told a scrum of reporters after the game. "My motto has always been to go as hard as you can for as long as you can. I relied mostly on my fastball. I didn't shake Carter off once. I wouldn't have worried if I'd given up one hit. What I really wanted was the win and a complete game, the first one that I've had since I've been with this team. I didn't get nervous from the sixth inning on because I knew in my mind that I wanted a no-hitter. I'm going to let this sink in. I've come a long way in less than one year. Last season at this time, I was pitching Double-A ball in Memphis."

After electing not to sign with the Mets in 1975, the Cardinals in 1976, and the White Sox in 1977 in order to attend Memphis State University in Tennessee, Lea had finally decided to sign with the Expos in 1978. He was called up from the Memphis Chicks midway through 1980 after he had posted a glittering 9–0 record and a 0.84 ERA. He finished out the 1980 season with a 7–5 record for the Expos.

On May 17, just one week after Lea's 1981 masterpiece, another Expos pitching prospect, Steve Ratzer, received bad news. He was released from the team after giving up a walk-off single to Jack Clark in a 5–4 Giants win in San Francisco.

When the season had started, the Expos had decided to give Ratzer a shot at the bigs, after several seasons of his turning heads in the minors. The young pitcher had been signed as a free agent out of St. John's University in Queens, New York, in 1975, and established quite a reputation as a solid minor-league pitching prospect, going 15–4 in 1980. He'd gone on to play for Escogido in the Dominican Republic winter league following that successful season. Ratzer was one of the stars for Escogido, which won the championship that year — the first time the team had ever won such a crown.

"Felipe Alou was the manager, Matty Alou coached third, Jesus Alou coached first, and Moises Alou was the bat boy," Ratzer said. "It was cool. I pitched really, really good. Tim Raines, Tim Wallach, and Jerry White were some of the guys on that team. And Pedro Guerrero of the Dodgers was our centre-fielder."

Then, after a short rest, Ratzer attended the Expos' 1981 spring-training session and won a spot; but he didn't last as long in Montreal as he wanted. On May 14, during a road trip to Los Angeles, the same Pedro Guerrero did some major damage to his winter-league teammate. "It was one of the last pitches I threw in the major leagues, a walk-off home run," Ratzer said. "I guess he knew what was coming. I threw him a good pitch and he still hit it out. It was the game where Fernando Valenzuela set a record with his eighth straight win as a rookie. I was sent down to Denver three days later. The Expos traded me for Jeff Reardon, and he took over my locker at Olympic Stadium, he took my uniform number, and he moved into my apartment — a beautiful one, on Mount Royal ... overlooking the city. I don't blame them for getting Jeff Reardon. I was not of Jeff Reardon's calibre. I was obviously a mediocre major-leaguer."

Ratzer never played another game in the majors, but he continued to play minor-league ball at various levels for several years before branching out into the restaurant business. He currently lives in Bluffton, South Carolina, where he's the pitching coach for Batters Box of Hilton Head Batting Cages.

Chapter 6

Did Valentine Not Want to Be Great?

What struck Expos trainer Ron McClain the most, the thing that he remembered more than anything about that historic Expos season of 1981, is about Number 17, one of the most talented players to ever put on an Expos uniform.

The fact [is] that Ellis Valentine kind of let the team down. He'd always say that if he wasn't one hundred percent, he wouldn't play. He'd say, "If I'm not a hundred percent, I won't play because the fans will boo me."

He'd refuse to play. He'd say, "I can't go today. I have sore legs or a sore knee or a sore hamstring or a sore groin." It was one thing after another. He always had to find out if he was able to play. If he was out the night before, then he probably wasn't going to play the next day. He hardly played. When he came to spring training in 1981, he was about 20 pounds overweight.

He was always complaining, sore this, sore that. He wouldn't play with soreness. He didn't want to do exercises.

> He didn't want to stay in shape. He didn't want to do the
> bicycle. We found out it had something to do with drugs.
> We found that out through other players.

There was at least one other incident that both Expos assistant trainer Mike Kozak and McClain remember about Valentine, not long before he was traded. That incident took place in Los Angeles. Players and coaches were shagging balls and batting practice was under way. Outfielder Rowland Office was standing near the batting cage and Valentine let loose with a long throw from the outfield.

"He hit Office on the fly. I think he was trying to tease him," Kozak said.

"He wanted to scare Office or make him jump away," McClain said. "Office didn't see it coming and it hit him square on the ankle. No bounce. From about 300 feet. He was too accurate. Rowland had just got out of the batting cage after BP. He was not even looking at Ellis in the outfield. Office was out six weeks. Then he had to run and hit for another week."

In an initial interview, Office remembered being hit by "one of the outfielders" and that he had just stepped out of the batting cage. In a subsequent interview, he acknowledged that it was Valentine who hit him. "I was coming out of the batting cage and got hit on the right ankle. Oh, yeah, it hurt, but it was an accident," Office told me. "We talked about it and we got over it. I don't think it was on purpose. I'd never experienced anything like that before. It was a lucky throw. I was running toward first and kept running, but the more I ran, the [sorer] it got and it got swollen. I went to the trainer's room and they took me to the hospital. I was there a couple of hours and they put a cast on it."

Just goes to show you how remarkable Valentine's strength was. "No question, he had the best arm in the National League," McClain said. "Better than Andre Dawson, Cesar Geronimo, Garry Maddox, Rick Monday. All of them. It's just that we couldn't get him to play regularly."

The Office incident took place somewhere between May 12 and May 14. Valentine was traded to the Mets on May 29 in exchange for Jeff Reardon, Dan Norman, and a player to be named later. Valentine was on the disabled list with a left hamstring injury when he was traded and didn't play for the Mets until June 5.

"I wasn't surprised he was traded, because he wouldn't play," McClain said.

Was the Office incident one of the factors in Valentine being traded?

"Yes," McClain said.

"They got Jeff Reardon out of me. Look at what he went on to do as a closer," Valentine told me in the 1990s. "I was really hurt by the trade, very confused. They had every right to be fed up with me. They put up with me because of my awesomeness. They put up with all the bullshit because of my talent."

To this day, Valentine alludes to his arm, and on his Twitter page he has a *Montreal Gazette* Aislin cartoon of himself with a ball coming out of a cannon. It's that arm that truly fascinated teammates such as Jerry White and Larry Parrish.

"I admired Valentine. The potential you saw in him, he was amazing. To see film of him, I get chills in my back and body," White said. Said Parrish,

> I played and coached a long time and I've never seen an arm like Ellis Valentine's from the outfield. It's just that the ball came out of there like a cannon when he threw it. I tell you, the other team watched him take infield and watched him throw. It would never happen for anyone else. The other team stayed out and watched him throw as they were shagging balls, and I mean he could just throw it and the ball looked like it was going to bounce and gravity never took hold. The ball kept coming on the same line.
>
> I remember in West Palm Beach, in A-ball, I swear that the ball took off like a jet. It was coming in and it sort of hit an air pocket and started rising. I swear the first-baseman could have cut it off, and then it went over the catcher's head. You know, I'm still friends with Ellis, and I think Ellis would be the first one to tell you that he had so much talent and it sort of slipped away from him. He was so young and he just did some foolish things when he was younger.
>
> I tell you, with Ellis ... Andre Dawson went to the Hall of Fame, and to me, Ellis had more talent than

Andre Dawson. There wasn't anything he couldn't do. For whatever reason, it's hard to understand. There is psychological stuff that gives a guy so much drive but with some others, they don't quite have it. I've heard Ellis say that he didn't want to be great, that he just wanted to be good and be left alone. For whatever reason, I think Ellis almost didn't like that he had so much talent, that so much was expected of him, that they expected him to be a superstar. Was he afraid to be good? You don't know. He was loaded with talent. Somehow, it slipped away.

As most people recall, Valentine may have been spooked at the plate after he was drilled in the face in St. Louis by a Roy Thomas pitch in 1980. The story goes that Valentine was high on cocaine when the pitch came in and that he just froze. McClain, according to Valentine, was the only person who visited him in hospital. And when he spent more time at Montreal General Hospital, Parrish came to spend time with him.

"I'll never forget Larry for that. I have good feelings for him. He was blond, all-American, tall and handsome, but he was just a regular kind of guy," Valentine said in the 1990s.

"You don't know how that affects a guy," Parrish said to me about the beanball by Thomas. "Some guys get right back in there like nothing happened. Some guys, it's always in the back of their minds. Paul Blair, after he got hit, tried to stay in there. I don't believe any hitter that plays never has a bit of fear up there. There are times you just don't see a pitcher good and his ball explodes."

Valentine didn't consent to an interview for this book, but he told me in the 1990s that a chronic ailment, "I-S-M," had been controlling him. As he put it,

It was I, Self, and Me. I went from the penthouse to the outhouse. I was selfish; I lived for me and Ellis. There were a lot of drug problems with the Expos, but I was the worst of all. I was such a whipping boy. I knew I had

49

a problem, but if I'd spoken up about it, I would've been blackballed. If I'd opened up, I was done. Drugs made me feel different. I didn't like Ellis Valentine. I never grew up. I was selfish.

It's just that I felt practice hurt me. There was no need to practise. I did not need practice. I was so gifted, I took that for granted. If you went out for practice before games, they'd work your asses off. I was totally out of control. Celebrity-ism is a disease. I had a real chance of being a good player for a very long time. I was a tremendously gifted ballplayer. My life was wicked, terrible, negative, disgusting. The drugs and booze were so much a problem. It was my behaviour, the way I acted.

Long-time executive Jim Fanning, who helped bring Valentine along from the minors through to the majors with the team, once said this about Valentine: "The greatest talent we ever saw. He was a great talent. I don't know how great he could have been. He had a sixth sense on how to play the game."

Valentine boasted a cocktail of talents, a five-tool mixture of concoctions: he could run, he could hit for average, he could hit for power, he could throw, and he could field. But his desire to be smug, confrontational, and arrogant turned the cocktail sour. Many times, he would show up late, but Williams would still put him in. Williams knew that the Expos were a better team with Valentine in the lineup.

Valentine turned his life around in the mid-to-late 1980s and got off drugs, but it was too late: his path to Cooperstown was closed.

"What a shame. He had everything," former Expos majority-owner Charles Bronfman said in 2017. "He was a great hitter. It was a waste of talent. I remember he could throw from the outfield to home plate without a bounce. He never hit the cutoff man. I knew about his injuries, but I found out later about the drugs."

Yes, Valentine was Cooperstown-calibre talent; but he got to show it for only a short time.

Chapter 7

Season Torn Apart by Strike

T he strike of 1981 was the talk of North America; not just Canada or sports America, but corporate America.

Baseball players and their union, through highly touted executive director Marvin Miller, confronted commissioner Bowie Kuhn, major-league owners, and chief negotiator Ray Grebey over free-agency compensation, an issue that had been bandied about for several years prior to that season.

Memories of Curt Flood, Andy Messersmith, and 1975 Expos pitcher Dave McNally lurked in the background. They had challenged baseball's archaic free-agent system a decade earlier with mixed results. Flood, in particular, drew attention by challenging baseball in a lawsuit. In a nutshell, teams then essentially owned players for the lifetime of their employment, which nowadays seems ludicrous.

At one point, Kuhn had said, "We will give in to the union over my dead body."

By 1981, the players' union finally drew the line and promised that the players would strike. There had been a glimpse of the trouble ahead in 1980 when the players shut down spring training for a week. Some 15 months later, as June came around again, the players remained steadfast that this time they would set up picket lines. On June 12, the ballparks went dark and the concession stands ceased operations.

The owners had taken out strike insurance and had no serious interest in negotiating. Expos player representative Steve Rogers was one of the key players involved in the negotiating process, along with Steve Renko, Ted Simmons, Mark Belanger, Buck Martinez, Phil Garner, and Doug DeCinces.

"The owners were prepared to let the strike insurance go until it ran out," recalled Don Fehr, general counsel with the Major League Baseball Players Association (MLBPA) until he took over the top job from Miller in 1985. He continued,

> What I remember is that management would make a decision when it was ready. The owners' strike insurance lasted something like 50 days. We met several times a week, sometimes more than once a day, but not after June 20 when Marvin went across the country to meet players from different teams.
>
> The owners essentially provoked the strike. The owners wanted to set a player value on free agency. If a team lost a premium free agent, then the owners wanted that team to receive a player of similar value or close to it. They wanted the compensation to be so high. That would have destroyed free agency. The players would never make that deal.

As the owners and player representatives negotiated, most players had to find something else to do.

Expos reliever Jeff Reardon remembers the strike for something more personal and sad. "I watched my father die," Reardon told me, grimly.

Tim Wallach, just months into his job as a part-time freelancing rookie with the Expos, went back home to California, where he worked unloading trucks for $7.57 per hour.

Sophomore Bill Gullickson returned home to Kankakee, Illinois, to work in his father's store, Don's Tires. Gullickson was born in Marshall, Minnesota, but his father had moved to Joliet, Illinois, to take a job when

Bill was nine years old. "It was an occupation. I'd just fiddle around the store," Gullickson said of that work. "You didn't know if the strike would last an hour, ten days, or a hundred days."

Rookie sensation Tim Raines went back home to Sanford, Florida, to work out with friends, somewhat frustrated because he was on a tear on the base-paths leading up to the strike. Raines was going head-to-head with Dodgers pitcher Fernando Valenzuela for top freshman honours. If there had been no strike, Raines could have challenged Lou Brock's NL record of 118 stolen bases, logged in 1974 with the St. Louis Cardinals. Raines could also have challenged the modern-day major-league record of 130 set by Rickey Henderson of the Oakland A's in 1982. As it turned out, Raines would steal 71 in only 88 games in 1981. Quite an achievement. "I had 50 stolen bases in 55 games when the strike came," Raines recalled in late July of 2017.

Back home in Haines City, Florida, the one Expos player who actually benefitted from the strike was third-baseman Larry Parrish, whose wrist injury from May of 1980 had never properly healed. But man, this resting period in the summer of 1981 did his wrist a world of good.

> The 1981 strike didn't help anyone in baseball other than me. I had a great 1979 season and in 1980 I was off to the best start I had ever had. On May 2 … at a home game against the Giants, I hit a double my first time up on a breaking ball on the outside of the plate. In my next at-bat, I was trying to not be leaning out over the plate in a typical baseball competition. But in the shadows of Montreal, the shadows were real tough during day games. Pitchers would lose a baseball and a lot of batters would get hit pretty hard. This particular pitch I didn't see. Ed Whitson wasn't nasty, but he was behind me in the count and the pitch was up and in. I didn't see it. I jerked my left hand off the bat into my chest so the ball wouldn't hit me. But it hit me on the right wrist; wound up breaking a little bone on the inside. It didn't break on the outside but broke close to my thumb. It didn't get better. I struggled with it the rest of the '80 season. I thought, hopefully, over winter, it would

be fine. But it didn't [heal]. Right before the strike, I saw an Expos doctor in San Francisco and he basically told me there were a lot of little bones in there and he didn't feel comfortable operating. He said that if I was an accountant he could operate, but [me] being a baseball player in the public eye, that he didn't want to try it. I told him it only hurt when I swung the bat. The doctor thought that, with me being in the prime of my career, I might have to look for another occupation. Two days after that, I was working with the cows and the cattle pens in Florida. I started swinging a hammer every day for six weeks in the family business. I didn't realize it was doing something good for my hand. The doctor said to keep swinging the hammer because it kept pushing blood to my wrist. I was swinging the hammer right-handed. I came back after the strike and the wrist didn't hurt anymore. I didn't have an issue with it after that. I was very lucky.

Even announcers Dave Van Horne and Duke Snider kept busy during the strike. Expos general manager John McHale devised a plan to allow fans to follow baseball in some way. In place of major-league games, Van Horne and Snider called minor-league games at the Triple-A level. "John wanted to keep baseball on people's minds, so Duke and I spent 38 days with the Indianapolis Indians, doing their games," Van Horne recalled.

While the strike was going, players weren't allowed to work out at Olympic Stadium and they weren't allowed to get treatment from McClain and assistant Mike Kozak. What the trainers decided to do to kill some time was to do some painting. "I was just getting ready to move," McClain recalled. "Mike and I spent most of six days painting the new apartment on Sherbrooke Street in Montreal. The furniture truck came a week late. Then my wife of six months and I moved in and that took a few days."

It was during the strike, on July 13, that Harry Renaud made the decision to leave the team after 13 years as the club's secretary-treasurer, controller, and chief financial officer. He had wanted to leave long before that but had stayed on out of a sense of loyalty. He just didn't feel comfortable. "I was hired in 1968, one of the first employees overall. It was a strange relationship. Charles Bronfman was the owner but I was reporting to John McHale." Any time Renaud needed money for organizational funding, he merely asked McHale, Bronfman, and the board of directors and they'd cut him a cheque.

"I was there struggling for 13 years, responsible for the business operations. I would go to Expos owners' meetings and give them financial updates," Renaud said. "I was in my 40s, wondering what I was going to do for the rest of my life. I was not the baseball guy needed to take over from John McHale. I was not fluently bilingual to stay in Quebec. I was not much of a baseball person.

"I was very close with Chris Speier of the Expos. I spent a lot of time with him, but it was awkward to be in management socializing with players."

At the winter meetings in December 1980, Renaud had given notice to McHale and Bronfman that he wanted to move on, but they twisted his arm and he stayed around until July 1981. Then he took a lucrative job in Vancouver, British Columbia, as the head of the Pacific National Exhibition. "The PNE had established poor business procedures and we went in and doubled PNE sales in two years," Renaud said. "We went in and counted napkins, plates, etc. After Vancouver's World Fair Expo 86, I stayed on to do consulting work for the PNE's concessions operations."

When the strike smoke cleared on July 29, there was a compromise of sorts in place. Teams that lost a "premium" free agent could be compensated from a pool of players left unprotected by all of the clubs. In return, the players agreed to have free agency restricted to players with six or more years of service.

"I think it was an acceptable deal and vastly, vastly better than agreeing to what the owners wanted, which would have destroyed free agency," Fehr said. "The deal was far from perfect, but under the circumstances it seemed like a good deal for the players."

Along the way, there was no love lost between the two sides. Grebey and Miller declined to shake hands when an agreement was finally reached. "It was pretty mean and ugly," Fehr remembered about the general tone of the negotiations.

"It was warfare back then," said player agent Tom Reich. "We agents weren't a formal part of the union, but we were very much involved. The union did a tremendous job. There is no way that the players would have accepted the compensation plan as proposed by the owners."

How imperfect was that season? While the Expos reconvened in West Palm Beach and players from other teams got in shape for the second half, the owners and union officials agreed that the division winners of each part of the split season would meet in a league division series. That meant that, even before play resumed on August 10, the Los Angeles Dodgers, Philadelphia Phillies, New York Yankees, and Oakland A's each had a play-off spot sewn up because they had sported the best records in their divisions at the time the strike took place. Weird but true.

"The split-season decision was collectively bargained. We had to agree on that," Fehr said. "That was part of the settlement. We thought that it was a good idea, to enhance the pennant races with another round of playoffs."

The night before play resumed in the second half of this aborted season, the All-Star Game was held in Cleveland. Gary Carter of the Expos was voted most valuable player after hitting two solo home runs. Teammates Andre Dawson and Tim Raines also got playing time.

Now, the real games could begin.

Chapter 8

Tommy Hutton Released

I n September of 1981, when the Expos saw that Tommy Hutton wasn't producing as he had in the past, they made a change.

Hutton got the news he was expecting, yet at the same time not expecting, on September 4, in mid-afternoon at Olympic Stadium, before a game against the Astros. "I was called out of batting practice and I went to the dugout bench and I sat between Dick Williams and John McHale," Hutton recalled. "I kinda knew what they were going to tell me. They told me that they were releasing me. I was awful that year. I had three hits. It was such a different game then compared to what it is now. Dick had such a set lineup. I was a decent player most of my career, but not that year. They wanted to make room for a right-handed bat in Bob Pate."

Pate was a highly touted piece of Expos property, at least on paper. He was on the front of a Topps-issued card from 1981 entitled "Expos Future Stars." On the card with him were Bobby Ramos and Tim Raines. I have that card somewhere. Pate had spent a good portion of his Expos career in Denver Triple-A, where he produced consecutive RBI seasons of 78, 63, and 65. He had made the big-league club in 1980, briefly, and hit .256.

But Hutton had done everything asked of him during his major-league career. Platoon player. Spot starter. Freelancer. Part-time player. Backup player. Cheerleader. Head of the Expos' Broke Underrated Superstars club, affectionately known as BUS, a reference to the part-timers who would make long trips to spring-training games while the regulars stayed behind at base camp in Daytona Beach or West Palm Beach.

"On a personal level, I had it in my mind to plan ahead for after baseball as a player," Hutton said. "John McHale knew I was interested in broadcasting. John asked if I wanted to remain with the club and do some broadcasting. At that time, they had Dave Van Horne and Duke Snider doing radio, but Ron Reusch was by himself when he was on the radio when Dave and Duke did television."

Hutton went home and talked over the situation with his wife and they agreed that he would take the job. It was a quick transition. The previous year, Hutton had sent letters to various clubs telling them that he would be interested in broadcasting if opportunities came up.

"I was appreciative of what John McHale did for me," Hutton said. "So I did 10 to 15 games that year in the broadcast booth. It was kind of good news/bad news. The good news was that I was looking forward to a new career, but the bad news was that I was a little jealous that I wasn't on the field doing my part to help my teammates."

Hutton would go on to spend 34 years in the broadcast booth, including long stints with the Blue Jays and Marlins. He has resided the last 35 years in the same house in Palm Beach Gardens, Florida. He lives close to Van Horne and former teammates Jeff Reardon and Bill Gullickson. "On a good day, with a good arm, I could throw a baseball into Gully's backyard," Hutton quipped.

Chapter 9

Williams Fired, Fanning Hired

The date was September 6, 1981, and John McHale was pacing in his room mid-morning at the Philadelphia Hilton. He would sit down, he would stand up; he would walk around pondering the slump his Expos were in. He was wondering what to do to shake up the club, and the main focus of his concentration was manager Dick Williams.

The Expos under Williams were floundering, currently in the throes of a 4–6 funk after a five-game winning streak in late August. It just so happened that September 6 was the day the New York Yankees fired manager Gene Michael and replaced him with Bob Lemon. McHale must have noticed or heard of this firing by bombastic Yankees owner George Steinbrenner.

Back in Montreal, Expos farm director Jim Fanning was at his Olympic Stadium desk when his phone rang. It was McHale. The two had been friends and allies going back to 1961 when they'd both worked for the Milwaukee Braves. McHale had been Milwaukee's GM in 1964 and he'd hired Fanning as assistant GM later that season after Fanning had moved up from smaller roles in the organization.

In unison, they moved with the Braves to Atlanta when the Milwaukee franchise was transferred there following the 1965 season. Then they both worked in the baseball commissioner's office for a period of time in the late 1960s. McHale was a chief aide to Commissioner William Eckert and Fanning was the first director of the Central Scouting Bureau.

In the fall of 1967, Fanning had actually been listed to be a coach for the Braves for the 1968 season, but at the winter meetings in Mexico City that December, six representatives from other major-league teams approached Braves GM Paul Richards to seek permission to talk with Fanning for the job with the Scouting Bureau, a position he eventually accepted.

Once installed, Fanning's new duties took him to New York, where he would often run into McHale, who was also based in the Big Apple. So, drawing on their familiarity and friendship, McHale asked Fanning if he wanted to come to Montreal, where McHale had just been named the expansion team's first president, to assist him in getting the new team started in the summer of 1968. Fanning quickly accepted. Now, 20 years after McHale and Fanning had first crossed paths in 1961, McHale was once again on the phone making another request of Fanning. The discussion came on a day the Expos lost 4–3 to the Phillies.

"Do you want to be the Expos' manager?" McHale asked Fanning, who couldn't believe what he was hearing.

"John called me one day and told me that he didn't like the way things were going and that he was thinking of making a change with the manager and that he wanted me to be the manager," Fanning recalled a few years ago. "He told me that if he felt the same way [on September 7] he would give me a call and that I would take over the club. When he asked me, absolutely, oh man, I made the decision in a flash that I would take the job.

"So he called me the next day [the seventh] and said he wanted me to take over and he told me to make arrangements to go to Philadelphia the next day, September 8, at noon, when he would make an announcement. I was very surprised and very excited. Gene Kirby, the travelling secretary, set up a flight for me in Montreal to go to Philadelphia."

Ironically, on September 7, the day McHale and Fanning made the agreement that Fanning would take over, the Expos won 5–4 under Williams.

On September 8, about 9:30 in the morning, two days after he first talked with Fanning, McHale met with Williams to tell him he was being let go. In essence, Williams's template was no longer working.

The 1981 Expos, sometime after Jim Fanning replaced Dick Williams as manager. Bat boys seated are Tino DiPietro and Frank Albertson. Front row, left to right, are Tim Raines, Steve Rogers, Steve Boros, Ozzie Virgil, Pat Mullin, Jim Fanning, Galen Cisco, Vern Rapp, Norm Sherry, Woodie Fryman. Second row: Bobby Ramos, Chris Speier, Gary Carter, Stan Bahnsen, Andre Dawson, Scott Sanderson, Ray Burris, Larry Parrish, Bill Lee, Bill Gullickson, Elias Sosa, assistant trainer Mike Kozak, travelling secretary Peter Durso, equipment manager Harvey Stone. Third row: assistant equipment manager John Silverman, Anthony Johnson, Jerry White, Grant Jackson, Mike Phillips, Warren Cromartie, Jeff Reardon, Rowland Office, David Palmer, John Milner, Jerry Manuel, head trainer Ron McClain. Back row: Tom Wieghaus, Terry Francona, Tim Wallach, Dave Hostetler, Charlie Lea, Tom Gorman, Bryn Smith, Pat Rooney, Wallace Johnson, Brad Mills, Dan Briggs, Rick Engle.

"One of the reasons for my decision was, we didn't feel we could win the way we were playing, with a lack of direction and discipline and questionable tactics," McHale said.

McHale noted that Williams had done "a lot of good things. He knew how to win." But since the strike had ended, Williams had "lost some of that." The Expos GM elected to go with Fanning because if he had chosen to bring in a "name" manager at that late stage in the season, it would have meant having to give the new man a long-term commitment. McHale also said he didn't want to promote a coach like Steve Boros because it wouldn't allow him enough time to show what he could do.

"The real reason, as I recall, that Dick was let go, was that in management's opinion he wasn't able to lead the team to the second-half victory.

Period," majority-owner Charles Bronfman told me in 2017. "When John replaced Dick, I was very much onside. I thought it was a good idea. John and I talked about it. Dick had just run out of gas as far as the team was concerned."

The first person Fanning called after the bombshell chat with McHale was his girlfriend, Marie Malandra. "In 1981, Jim and I had been dating five years," Fanning's wife told me, recalling that time. "He called me up that week in September and said there was something he had to discuss with me. He came over and told me that Williams was going to be let go as the team's manager. He said John McHale would be hiring someone new."

As the conversation evolved, curiosity got the best of Marie. "I asked Jim who it might be. 'It might be me,' he said. 'In fact, it is me.'

"I congratulated him," she said. "He told me it meant that he would be with the team travelling and spending even longer hours at the ballpark. And that it meant the time we could spend together would be drastically reduced. I told him I understood the nature of the game and the intense role of manager. I also told Jim, 'I will support you in everything you have to do.' He replied, 'That's all I needed to hear.'"

It was a peculiar move by McHale, because Fanning hadn't managed at any level since the 1962 Class-A season in Eau Claire, Wisconsin.

"The nice thing was that when I took over the club, a good part of it was developed by the Expos and I had had a hand in it," Fanning said. "I would have 65 percent of the club in the palm of my hand because I had a hand in signing a lot of them, from Carter to Dawson to Gullickson, David Palmer, Scott Sanderson, and others. It was a very comforting thought.

> Nineteen eighty-one was a fantastic season. Canada, Montreal, and the fans were treated to awesome baseball by the Expos, under the leadership of their manager, Jim Fanning. Winning the only Divisional Championship in Expos' history, and just one step away from the World Series. It was magic!
> — Marie Fanning, wife of Jim Fanning, in a 2017 prepared statement

"When I got to Philadelphia, I had a meeting with the players in the clubhouse and told them I had not asked for the job, the job came to me."

When asked whether any player stepped up and asked him anything, Fanning replied, "Nobody asked me a question."

There was no animosity between Williams and Fanning over the move. In fact, they remained good friends. When Williams was elected to the Hall of Fame in Cooperstown in 2008, he invited Fanning, who travelled to the ceremony as Williams's guest. Imagine. How nice that was. Williams brought along Fanning as a guest. Beautiful.

One of the biggest losers when the Expos fired Williams was second-baseman Rodney Scott. He didn't get as much playing time as he had under Williams.

"Rodney was one of Dick's favourite players," outfielder Rowland Office told me. "That was tough. We didn't see that coming at all. It was something out of the blue. Dick was a better manager than Jim Fanning. That was a wrong move. It kinda pissed off a few players. Jim put Rodney on the bench."

Yes, Williams just loved Scott. The lithe second-baseman couldn't hit worth a lick but he sure could run and he played tremendous defence.

FINDING OUT THE NEWS

It was September 8, 1981, and Bill Gullickson was in his hotel room in Philadelphia when a teammate called him on the phone.

"Did you hear they fired Dick Williams?" the guy asked Gullickson.

"No, holy cow. Who did they hire?" Gullickson asked.

"Jim Fanning," he was told.

"I couldn't believe Dick got fired," Gullickson said in 2017. "He was a really good manager. He was tough. I bore his wrath one time. I missed a sign in St. Louis and he took me aside and said that if I didn't learn signs that I'd be back in Denver. He didn't play favourites. I knew Jim from the minor leagues. He knew most of the personnel. It was a pretty smooth transition."

"Rodney was my favourite player," third-base coach Ozzie Virgil Sr. said close to 40 years later. "He was a very exciting player. He came to play. There wasn't a lot of punch in his bat, but he could steal second or third anytime. He could steal third without anyone knowing it. All of a sudden, he was at third."

From 1979 to 1981, Scott had played full-time for the Expos. In 1979, he hit .238 with three homers and 42 ribbies in 562 at-bats. In 1980, he hit .224 with zero homers and 46 RBI. In 1981, he hit .205 with no homers and 26 RBI. When Fanning came along, Scott's stock plummeted.

"I just felt it was strange to fire Dick Williams," Scott said in an interview in 2017. "I couldn't understand that. We were doing fine under Dick as far as I'm concerned. I had no control over it. You had to deal with it."

Back in 1981, Scott was quite blunt about his displeasure with Fanning taking over. "He can go to hell," Scott told *Le Journal de Montréal*, in a story that appeared September 11.

Chapter 10

Rogers Speaks Out
About Williams

A s other Expos weighed in on the 1981 Dick Williams/Jim Fanning scenario in 2017, Steve Rogers contributed an interesting idea. "Contract negotiations," he told me, stating that was the real reason Williams was let go. "Dick had been unhappy, and they didn't give him an extension. That was the undercurrent. Coming out of the strike, we got struggling and we were playing so-so. But the real reason was that the club didn't want to give Dick an extension. He had a disgruntled attitude."

Interestingly, this is how Dick Williams's son Rick reacted to Rogers's slant: "That's not right. Steve Rogers didn't know the real story."

But there it was, near the end of the regular season, and they fired Williams. Why? He was signed only through 1981, so it was natural that Williams would want an extension to take him into 1982 and longer. He had been with the Expos since 1977 and had almost completed his fifth full season when he was canned. You would have to think, though, that Williams had enjoyed a pretty good run with the Expos, in terms of longevity.

As Brodie Snyder wrote in his early 1980s book, *The Year the Expos Almost Won the Pennant!*, with the Expos, Williams was the first manager ever to earn $200,000 per season — pretty good coin in those days.

McHale was also dealing with a report by United Press International reporter Milton Richmond, who wrote that Williams had a deal to manage the Yankees in 1982. In his book *No More Mr. Nice Guy*, Williams said that those rumours linking him with the Yankees were what led McHale to fire him. The Yankees fired Gene Michael on September 6, the day McHale asked Fanning if he wanted to manage the Expos. The day before he was fired, Williams was being queried by Expos beat writers about rumours he was going to the Yankees.

Nevertheless, coaches like long-time Williams confidant Norm Sherry disliked McHale's decision at the time, and he still didn't like it when I talked with him in late 2016.

"Lousy. I didn't think it was right," said Sherry, who was Williams's third-base coach with the Expos that season and in subsequent seasons with the Padres. "He was running that ball club, and all of a sudden, they told him you can't do it?"

Bench coach Ozzie Virgil Sr. wasn't thrilled about Williams's being replaced either. Both Virgil and Sherry had long ties to Williams. Virgil coached under Williams in Montreal from 1977 to 1981 and Sherry was an understudy to Williams from 1978 to 1981. Not surprisingly, Virgil and Sherry followed Williams to San Diego in 1982 when he became manager of the Padres.

REASONS/SCENARIOS FOR DICK WILLIAMS'S FIRING

- Steve Rogers used as a pinch-runner August 31: punctured a lung and broke a rib.
- Stalled contract talks between disgruntled Dick Williams and management.
- Feud between Williams and closer Jeff Reardon.
- Williams's hard-nosed attitude toward players.
- Underachieving team was in a 4–6 funk.
- McHale heard Williams had a deal to go to the New York Yankees.
- Youppi! didn't want to be manager.

"Dick was the Angels' manager in 1976 and they fired him in the middle of the season. I was the third-base coach and they hired me to replace Dick," Sherry said. "I was surprised. I took his job when he got fired, and then he hired me to be a coach in Montreal in 1978."

Even Expos pitching coach Galen Cisco had a link to Williams because Cisco was a pitcher for Williams when he managed the Toronto Triple-A club in 1966 and was a pitcher for Williams when he managed the Red Sox in 1967. But Cisco didn't follow Sherry, Virgil, and Williams to San Diego right away. He stayed put in Montreal, but became Williams's pitching coach in San Diego in 1985.

Steve Rogers mentioned the stalled contract talks for Williams as an "undercurrent," but there were other undercurrents causing waves, and Rogers himself was part of one.

During a game on August 31, Williams inserted Rogers as a pinch-runner. This was odd, considering Rogers was the Expos' best pitcher. This was what McHale was referring to at the news conference announcing Williams's dismissal and Fanning's hiring. Remember the "questionable tactics" phrase? One such tactic obviously was Williams's decision to use Rogers as a pinch-runner.

"I'll tell you something," Rogers said to me. "Dick didn't want to use a position player, so he put me in to pinch-run. I had to slide and I tried to reach back on first base and I think I hit the wrist. I couldn't catch my breath. I go to the locker room, go in the shower, and Woodie Fryman is showering there. 'Man, Woodie, I can't breathe.'

"I started to cough, big cough. There was a circle of blood splatters on the bottom of the shower. This is not good. I coughed up a huge amount of blood. I broke a rib and punctured my left lung. I had trouble breathing."

Rogers did not think that Williams using him as a runner was a factor in McHale getting rid of him.

"So they made a change and chose Jim," Rogers said. "They were going with an encyclopedia of a Montreal Expo in Jim Fanning. He was the embodied baseball lifer, dedicated beyond belief. His experience in the middle of a pennant race was a bit iffy, but the move worked."

Larry Parrish had his own opinion about the situation:

> We were very surprised when Dick was fired.
>
> Dick was an old-school-type manager. He wasn't friendly with his players. Being old-school, it was his belief to keep a distance between you and the players. He wasn't what you would call a friendly type guy; but, at the same time, he came to us with a big reputation in the game. As soon as he got here, we got better. It was a major deal to get rid of a man of his stature. They thought we were underachieving and that we needed a change.
>
> With Jim, it was different. It wasn't really uncomfortable having him because he'd been in the Expos system for a long time. We were familiar with Jim. It was probably an easier transition because we knew the guy and he knew us. We weren't total strangers.

Just days before Williams was fired, Expos backup pitcher Tommy Hutton had been let go.

"I used to tell people my opinion of Dick Williams," Hutton said. "Dick had that set lineup and there would be two or three weeks where he wouldn't even talk to you, contrary to other managers I worked around. I remember being around Jim Leyland when he managed the Marlins. He would talk to every player during every BP. He said guys who aren't playing need to have someone to talk to them. You know, Dick wasn't the greatest people person, but I admired him because he was a great tactician and a strategizing manager."

There were reports at the time that one of the reasons McHale fired Williams was a feud between Williams and pitcher Jeff Reardon, who didn't think he was getting enough work. Williams even singled out Reardon and mentioned that scenario in his book, *No More Mr. Nice Guy.*

"Dick Williams was an asshole," Reardon told me. "I was pissed off at him. He said in his book that I'd go crying to the front office about not being used. It was just a bunch of bullshit. It was the furthest thing from the truth. I'm not going to go to John McHale and complain about him not using me."

Whatever the case, others chimed in about the managerial change.

"Poor Jim, he was a little overmatched," 1981 call-up Dan Briggs said in 2017. "There were a couple of times when Jim forgot that you can't go out to the mound twice in the same inning to talk to the pitcher. If you go the second time, you have to replace the pitcher. We had to tackle Jim. There would be nobody warmed up in the bullpen. He was a fun-loving, a kind of cheerleader-type guy, really different than Dick. Shortly after I was called up, Dick installed me at first base and put Warren Cromartie on the bench. Cromartie was having a feud with Williams and Cromartie really raised a big stink in the paper. Next day, I was back on the bench, and shortly after, Williams was fired."

Speaking of Cromartie, he blatantly denounced the move to fire Williams, both on September 12, 1981, and close to 40 years later. "I have no respect for him [Fanning]," Cromartie told *La Presse* a few days after Fanning's hiring.

"Dick taught us, he took us under his wing," Cromartie told me in 2017. "It was really great to get a manager of his calibre. We knew he was a leader. The team was very disappointed with the move to fire Dick. We were playing to win this for Dick. We were very upset. We decided to dedicate the rest of the season to him. We took it upon ourselves to put it all together for Dick. We weren't playing for the new manager. We got shafted by the front office."

Expos icon Andre Dawson wasn't about to take sides in the confab, opting for a more neutral observation: "I always appreciated Dick Williams as a manager. Jim Fanning, too."

"I'm pretty sure that Dick Williams might have been the best manager I've ever seen, and they let him go," umpire Joe West told me. "You had the general who led you there. Their biggest mistake was letting Williams go. It was so stupid. I'm not a manager. I'm an umpire. But he was probably the best manager I've ever seen. Dick and I would argue tooth and nail over calls, but we were still friends."

Like Reardon, an unexpected beneficiary of Jim Fanning's hiring was rookie Bryn Smith.

In the latter stages of a pennant race, little did Smith think he would get to pitch much, if at all, after he was called up from Denver Triple-A. But, sure enough, because Fanning had been the Expos' farm director, he was familiar with what Smith could do. In fact, it was Fanning who told Smith many months before that he needed another pitch to survive in the major leagues. The pitch Smith came up with was the palmball, something he referred to as a "slopball."

At 26, Smith was an "old" rookie, but he had won 15 games that season in Denver under manager Felipe Alou and deserved a call-up. The palmball sure helped out. For that pitch, the ball is placed tightly in the palm or held between the thumb and ring finger and thrown as a quasi-fastball, but slower, throwing batters off balance a little. Other major-leaguers, such as Bob Stanley, Dave Giusti, Ray Culp, and Satchel Paige, also used the palmball as part of their arsenal. Smith went on to an 81–71 record in his career with the Expos through the 1989 season, thanks in part to that palmball, which, oddly enough, he already had in his repertoire long before Fanning recommended a new pitch.

> I had the palmball since high school. The thing is, I didn't realize how good it was. It was the third pitch, probably the best pitch I knew how to use, as far as timing. The biggest thing was that Fanning recommended that I go and play winter ball in 1980 in Maracaibo, Venezuela, for two months. He said winter ball would be a great thing for me. I went down there and had success against major-league hitters. Hitters would tell me I had a great change-up. I could throw the pitch anytime I wanted. Okay, I said. Wow!
>
> Because of my success in Venezuela, I was invited to spring training in 1981. Had I not gone to winter ball and had success, I probably would not have been invited.... That was kind of the last thing, my last chance. It was my eighth year in professional ball, seven years in the minors. At that point, I was going to be released, or out of baseball, or be kept and used. I truly believe all things happen for a reason.

Smith was called up September 1, 1981, and entered his debut game in the fourth inning in relief of starter Scott Sanderson. He threw two-thirds of an inning, giving up no runs. He got Keith Moreland to hit into a double play.

What happened was that we were going to Omaha to Denver and then to Philadelphia. We were called up the day after we won the Triple-A title. So my first game in the major leagues was September 8, when they fired Dick Williams. I didn't expect to pitch. It was great to be there. I didn't realize Fanning's familiarity with me, so I got used [in the game]. I wasn't expecting to come and pitch any of those games. So Fanning and I were out on the mound with Gary Carter, and Fanning said, "Don't be afraid to use the funny pitch."

So Fanning leaves the mound and Carter asked me, "What is the funny pitch?" I said it was my change-up. I can throw it anytime.

One more thing, my fastball and my sinker were a lot like my palmball, and Tony Gwynn told me one time the palmball was hard to pick up and hard to hit. He was a .440 hitter against me and had so much success against me, so for him to say that, it was something. The palmball had some movement on it. It would come out of the hand and just fade away against both right-handed and left-handed hitters. It was a bonus.

Like most of the call-ups that fall, though, Smith didn't dress for any of the playoff games.

We clinched, we went back up to Montreal, and Jim had to make a roster move to come to 25 players. So it was kind of between [me] and Stan Bahnsen. He had a hamstring problem. I was taken off the roster and I went back home. So I went to California and stayed ready. I was still working out. In the Dodgers series, Stan had the hamstring injury and wasn't used. The nice thing was that I got free tickets to the Dodgers-Expos games in Los Angeles. I lived three hours away.

I liked all of the guys that year. They took me under their wing, and most of all Warren Cromartie, who was a kind of a big rock-and-roll fan, a huge Rush fan. Cro started to tip the clubhouse guys and he started buying me shirts. He couldn't stand the shirts I was buying.

I was grateful and thankful for what Woodie Fryman did. He made sure I did my running. He taught me a great work ethic. He was always the first one to the ballpark. He'd watch when I got to the park and then he would ask if I ran hard enough.

One person who was taken aback by the Williams firing was Williams's son Rick. He had been a left-handed pitcher in the Expos' minor-league system for a number of years, but at the time his father was fired, he was doing something different for the organization.

"I have a number of memories about that. The first thing was the disappointment," Rick Williams said.

I was in the instructional league as an instructor. It was awkward and uncomfortable. Bob Gebhard, the Expos' director of player development at the time, instructed me not to hold grudges, that I had to watch out for my career. I could have gone in the other direction and been mouthy. I worked my way through the firing.

It appeared the Yankees had wanted my dad for 1982, and that was the reason the Expos let him go, but it didn't turn out that way. He didn't go to New York. In retrospect, there is an obvious shelf life with being a manager. The front office tuned him out and it was time to move to the next setting. I was old enough to know that feeling was happening.

Chapter 11

The Biggest Triple in Expos History

After 15 years in the big leagues, Canada received its first baseball prize when the Montreal Expos rallied to defeat the Mets 5–4 and clinched the second-half race in the National League's East Division. It was an emotional moment for the Expos because they had contested for the divisional title on the final weekend of the last two seasons and failed each time. But this time, four weeks after Jim Fanning replaced Dick Williams as manager, they rewrote a piece of their history.

> — Joseph Durso, sports reporter, *New York Times*, October 4, 1981

Wallace Johnson had arrived in the major leagues in early September of 1981 as a confident young man, just like some of his Triple-A Denver Bears teammates who were also called up. The Bears, under manager Felipe Alou, won the Pacific Coast League championship in 1981 and, all of a sudden, Johnson was in the bigs. He had been a prized prospect ever since he spun a major bat with the Indiana State University Hoosiers and prior to that with the Theodore Roosevelt High School team in his hometown of Gary, Indiana.

During the 1979 season, Johnson was some kind of hitter at Indiana State in Terre Haute, located some three hours from Gary. The second-baseman led the nation in hitting in NCAA play by batting just under .500. Yes, just a shade under .500. He finished at a splendid .491 with 78 hits, three homers, and 39 RBI in 159 at-bats. Whew. Do you think the Expos didn't take notice?

So a little over two years after he was drafted by the Expos, Johnson was in the big leagues along with a host of others. "There was Bryn Smith, Brad Mills. I'm looking at the picture on the wall. I'm going to say Dave Hostetler, Pat Rooney, Terry Francona," Johnson said. "Those are some of the guys who came up to the Expos that year. We were riding high, so getting called up was icing on the cake that season."

The gang of Expos newbies had been in the majors for only a few days when Dick Williams was fired and replaced by Jim Fanning. As rookies just getting called up, "We just kept our mouths shut," he said about the managerial change. But no doubt about it, Fanning knew Johnson like the back of his hand. So in the first few weeks he was with the Expos, Johnson's contribution was limited.

When the Expos went to New York in early October for a series against the Mets, Johnson called his good friend Clef Santiago to pass the time.

It was October 2, 1981, the night before a Saturday matinee between the Expos and Mets at Shea Stadium, and "Clef and I were reminiscing. He was a big Yankees fan," Johnson recalled in 2017. "He was a college friend I knew. I always knew he was my welcoming committee to New York. We were talking about how hard the Expos were battling. That was the buildup to the Mets series."

The next day, a win by the Expos would give them their first-ever berth in post-season action.

The Mets took a 3–0 lead early on, but the Expos came back to win it 5–4, thanks to some heroics — by Johnson! He had been sitting on the bench surrounded by Gary Carter, Bill Gullickson, Warren Cromartie, and assistant equipment manager John Silverman. Johnson even sent me a photo of the actual scene of that group just mentioned — moments before he "was summoned to pinch-hit."

"Jim Fanning called my name. It was a surprise," Johnson recollected. "I had to jump up."

All of a sudden, Johnson was pinch-hitting for pitcher Bill Lee. Not an easy task, this role of pinch-hitter. Here he was, a rookie going up against an experienced reliever in Neil Allen. But Johnson was more than capable. He fouled off pitch after pitch, many of them thrown outside, all fastballs.

"It's Shea Stadium, the Mets had their ace reliever, who was one of the top relievers at the time," Johnson said. "He was the veteran trying to intimidate the rookie. I hit the ball where it wasn't expected — to right-centre. It was a 2–2 fastball. Allen was saying, 'Hey, this rookie is swinging too hard and I'm going to blow him away.' It was a big blow for me. I was flying around the bases going to third base. I knocked in two runs and we took the lead. I looked into the dugout and I saw my teammates jumping up and down. When I saw them doing that, I felt like I was accepted. It was a lifetime achievement. It was surreal."

You might have expected a star player to do what Johnson did, but here it was: the rookie did it.

"It was electrifying for Expos fans and the team. You always think that a Dawson or a Carter or a Wallach or someone like Parrish would get the big hit in that situation, but here it was Wallace Johnson. When he hit that triple, as he told you, he felt like he was a bona fide big-league player," Expos play-by-play man Dave Van Horne said in 2017.

> The Expos achieved their title on a cold and windy afternoon in Shea Stadium by overcoming a 3–0 Mets' lead inside three innings. The Expos finally edged in front in the seventh on a two-run, pinch-hit triple by Wallace Johnson, a 25-year-old certified public accountant from Gary, Ind., who joined the team as a rookie infielder two weeks ago.
> — Joseph Durso, *New York Times*

"Oh yeah, Wallace's hit, that was cool. It was a very clutch hit. Wallace will always be remembered for that," Bill Gullickson said.

"In the dugout, we were going crazy," Warren Cromartie said. "It really boosted our confidence. It was good to see guys like Wallace, Jerry Manuel, Jerry White, Rowland Office contributing. In the clubhouse, it was bedlam, it was crazy. It was actually a sad situation. Ellis Valentine had been traded to the Mets and he came into the clubhouse to see us."

Because of that triple, Johnson was no longer just a nobody in Gary, Indiana. That town produced the Jackson Five, with Michael Jackson banging the bongos. "The Jacksons grew up about five blocks away from me," Johnson said. "We all knew who they were, and my brother was in the same high school as one of the brothers. I remember Jermaine playing in the same Little League at the same time I did. I passed their house at 2300 Jackson Street on the way to the baseball field." But Johnson is part of Gary history now, too, his legacy that three-bagger.

"The two-run triple, it was symbolic of being called up to the major leagues, especially for a championship team," Johnson said as he chuckled.

Was it the highlight of his career? "It was the impetus of a career," he said. "You know what, everyone talks about the triple in a hostile environment at Shea Stadium, but it wasn't as big as the time I faced Ron Robinson of Cincinnati, who was pitching a perfect game in the ninth inning. I hit a single with two out in the ninth and Tim Raines behind me hit a home run. He lost his no-hitter and he lost his shutout."

That happened on May 2, 1988, at Riverfront Stadium in Cincinnati. Robinson had retired the first two batters in the ninth before Johnson, again a pinch-hitter, launched a soft liner to left in front of Kal Daniels. The Expos still lost 3–2, but Johnson was happy with what he had done.

But on that pennant-winning day in New York, the playoff-clinching save in relief of Steve Rogers went to Jeff Reardon, who had been traded to the Expos by the Mets in the Ellis Valentine transaction. There he was, Reardon, facing his old mates in a game that saw the Expos going to the post-season for the first time in their history.

"I was so excited saving that game against the team that traded me," Reardon said years later.

Reardon, ironically, had been drafted by the Expos back in 1973 out of Wahconah High School in Dalton, Massachusetts, where he was a national honours student, with mathematics "always my best subject." Yet, he didn't sign with the Expos because he had a scholarship to the University of Massachusetts. He admits his parents were "very poor" and that they really wanted him to sign with the Expos.

To get a better look at Reardon, the Expos sent several scouts to Dalton to see him pitch.

"Before they made an offer, they wanted to take one more look," Reardon said. "Tom (T-Bone) Giordano was the scout I was dealing with, and I threw that day to Barry Foote, the backup catcher. I remember breaking part of his mitt with my pitches. They really wanted to sign me. Somebody up there liked me. To get picked out of Massachusetts was really something. Usually, players in those days came from Florida or California."

Reardon did end up attending U Mass at Amherst and spent four years there, majoring in history, although he didn't go for academics, just "pretty much for baseball." After finishing college, he went undrafted before being signed by the Mets as a free agent in 1977.

It's kind of strange and ironic, because eight years later, after the Expos drafted me, I ended up in Montreal in the trade for Ellis Valentine. I had mixed feelings with the trade. I had spent two and a half years with the Mets. I had some awesome years with the Mets. I was pretty damn good. I saw an opportunity to be a closer in New York, but Neil Allen was a bonus baby and they had a lot of money invested in him.

But in Montreal, I saw the opportunity to do the job I wanted and that was to close out games. I went over there at the end of May and I was used as a setup man more than a closer. Dick Williams was the manager and maybe he figured I was too young to be the closer. They used guys like Woodie Fryman, Bill Lee, and different guys to close out the games. But when Dick was fired and Jim Fanning took over, the first thing Jim said was, "You're the closer." So I ended up saving six games there at the end of the season.

Of course, the sheer notion that the Expos had finally won a playoff berth was exhilarating for the players and prompted beat writer Brodie Snyder of the *Montreal Gazette* to pen a book titled *The Year the Expos Finally Won Something!* Even diehard Expos fan Donald Sutherland found his way into the clubhouse and was doused with champagne.

"It was extremely special. It was nice to pop champagne," winning pitcher Steve Rogers recalled.

"That was just a great, great feeling," Larry Parrish said, chuckling. "Until you've been there, it's hard to describe. If you're a horseracing buff like me, you follow horses, you see owners, trainers, and they're trying to talk to each other after winning a big race. You qualify for the Kentucky

HOSTETLER HIT ONE OF THE LONGEST HOME RUNS AT SHEA STADIUM

Dave Hostetler played five games with the Expos in 1981 and he will be best remembered for one of the longest home runs ever hit at Shea Stadium in New York, if not the longest.

And it was certainly one of the longest dingers ever hit by an Expo.

The blast off of Mets pitcher Pete Falcone came October 4 when the Expos fielded a decidedly Triple-A look because they had clinched a playoff spot the day before, thanks to Wallace Johnson's pinch-hit two-run triple.

"I can only remember the ball going over the bullpen in old Shea Stadium and landing in the parking lot," Hostetler recalled.

According to Mets public-relations guru Jay Horwitz, the ball had to have travelled over 500 feet if it made the parking lot. That ranks up there with some other long pokes at Shea by the likes of Tommie Agee and Dave Kingman.

As he rounded the bases, Hostetler was ecstatic, but when he reached the dugout he was surprised to see that there was no commotion, no high-fives. He was ignored. Rookie initiation had set in.

Derby. There's no way to describe the feeling you have in baseball, the feeling you get when you get into the playoffs. The further you go, the better it gets. Guys like Wallace you never forget."

Recalled Chris Speier: "Oh God, that was so great. We really partied on the plane and into the night."

When the game was over, the Expos got on a bus, went to the airport in New York, and flew to Dorval Airport in suburban Montreal, where one of life's great surprises took place: 10,000 people showed up to welcome them back home. Even the National Hockey League's Montreal Canadiens never garnered such support at the airport.

"It was in the evening. It was just getting dark because we had played a day game," Cromartie remembered. "It was a short flight to Montreal. We were on the bus and the people started serenading the bus and shaking the bus. They were starting to push the bus. They asked us to get out of the bus.

"They gave me the great silent treatment," Hostetler joked. "They treated it like nothing happened. Most of the starters were in the clubhouse because they did not play. But all were great after the game. I remember going 3-for-3. I was 3-for-6 and hit a cool .500 on the season.

"What the home run and the time I spent with the Expos did was give me a lot of confidence. It was quite a thrill for me to come up that season — one of the greatest experiences in my life. That team had a bunch of great guys, like Cromartie, Rogers, Carter — they all helped me a lot. You really learned a lot to see how those guys went about their business every day."

Hostetler had arrived in the big leagues after tearing up Triple-A with the Expos' farm team in Denver in 1981 with 27 homers and 103 RBI. Back in 1979, he hit 20 homers with 114 RBI at Double-A Memphis.

Hostetler was traded to the Texas Rangers late in spring training in 1982 along with Larry Parrish in exchange for Al Oliver. Hostetler hit 22 homers and collected 67 RBI with Texas but his star lost its shine thereafter.

It was absolutely a madhouse. Let me tell you, all hell broke loose. That was Montreal. Oh my God, the fans were everywhere, [even in] trees. It was unbelievable. So we got out of the bus. There was a little podium and some speeches were made."

Said Ray Burris, "That crowd showed you the passion that was exhibited in the community in Montreal. We were welcomed with loving arms. It was an overwhelming reception. That's what I felt. They came out showing their support. It was another element that gave us energy going forth."

Going forth into the upcoming series against the Phillies.

Left out in the cold that October were the Cincinnati Reds and St. Louis Cardinals. They missed out on a playoff run, despite boasting the best full-season records, because of the format agreed upon by the players association and the owners after the strike.

"A sad note about 1981 was the Reds had the best overall record in baseball that season, but under the format, they didn't make the playoffs," Expos play-by-plan man Dave Van Horne said. "I had a good friend in broadcasting with the Reds. His name was Jim Winters. I would kid him that the Expos were going to the playoffs. He was telling me that the Reds made up tumblers with Reds players' photos on them and they said 'Best Team in Baseball' over a 1981 pennant. When they didn't make the playoffs, Jim sent me about half a dozen of those tumblers."

Part Three

THE NATIONAL
LEAGUE
DIVISION SERIES

Chapter 12

Taking On the Phillies

F our days after Wallace Johnson's history-making triple, the Expos found themselves playing the Philadelphia Phillies. It has been called a mini-series, but officially it was one of two National League Division Series, the other involving the Los Angeles Dodgers and Houston Astros.

The Expos had to make some roster changes.

Tim Raines couldn't play a position and couldn't handle a bat, but the Expos kept him on their 25-man roster for the NLDS because he could still run and play havoc as a pinch-runner and a base-stealer. He had damaged his hand September 13, sliding into home plate head-first.

"Tim would have had a stoved finger or sprained thumb," recalled trainer Ron McClain.

Fancy word, that —*stoved*— meaning jammed.

"Yes, that is what they call it with fingers and thumbs," McClain said, smiling.

But Raines had started nine games against the Phillies during the regular season and had stolen 12 bases. No wonder the Expos wanted to keep him on the active roster.

Rodney Scott was left off because of a bruised shoulder suffered October 1, paving the way for Jerry Manuel to play second base. Also excluded was Rowland Office, who was still recovering from the broken ankle suffered in mid-May when Ellis Valentine drilled him with that 300-foot throw from the outfield during batting practice. "Because of the injury and the strike, Office simply never got his act together offensively," McHale told reporters at the time.

October 3 hero Wallace Johnson was kept on the roster, along with rookie pitcher Tom Gorman, a left-hander whose forkball both general manager John McHale and manager Jim Fanning liked. Gorman got the nod to replace Charlie Lea, who had a sore elbow.

Jerry White called the battle between the Expos and Phillies a "David and Goliath" confrontation. After all, the Phillies were the defending World Series champions.

"The Phillies had more experienced players," White said in 2017. "Those guys were huge. You're talking guys like Steve Carlton, Pete Rose, Bob Boone, Tim McCarver, Larry Bowa, Garry Matthews, Lonnie Smith, Keith Moreland, Mike Schmidt, and so on. To be on the field with those guys was really something, really satisfying."

BONING A BAT

Canadian Press photographer Bill Grimshaw believes the occasion may have been before an NLDS game in 1981 between the Phillies and the Expos.

Anyway, Grimshaw happened to see Phillies veteran Pete Rose down a hallway near the Phillies' clubhouse, conducting a ritual with his bat.

"I was looking for a picture," Grimshaw said. "He was rubbing his bat on a bone. It's like a dumb-bell. It's about a foot long. It's called boning the bat. A lot of players do it. So I asked Rose what the bone was for. So he explained it all."

"I took this bone out of [teammate] Bake McBride's hip," Rose told Grimshaw, joking.

"I almost shit my pants," Grimshaw said. "It's the funniest thing I saw in baseball."

The Expos had their own "Goliath" pitcher in Steve Rogers, who took it to the Phillies in Game 1, in the first major-league baseball playoff game ever held outside the U.S. The Expos won 3–1 as Rogers out-duelled lefty Steve Carlton, whose reputation at the time had reached mythical proportions. It was the 14th time Rogers and Carlton had met during their careers.

Rogers scattered eight hits before Jeff Reardon came on in the ninth inning to nail down the victory. Reardon retired all three batters he faced.

Doubles was the name of the game for the Expos. Gary Carter doubled home the first run, doubles by Tim Wallach and Chris Speier led to the second run, and Warren Cromartie's RBI two-bagger brought in the third run to counteract a home run by Keith Moreland.

The score was the same in Game 2, as Bill Gullickson worked 8.2 innings before giving way to Reardon. Phillies starter Dick Ruthven lasted only four innings. Carter hit a two-run homer and Speier was instrumental again with a single. Gullickson had the Phillies shut out before Smith doubled home Pete Rose, who had singled.

"They had guys like Rose, Schmidt, Boone, guys I watched on television when I was in high school," Gullickson recalled. "Then I got to play against them. I just tried to keep my composure. They had a lot of right-handed batters. The Phillies had a lot of experience and they had more experience later in the game when they got to see what you were throwing to them two or three times. Trying to get them out, it was a chess match. I was fortunate to have Steve Rogers to watch to see how he approached hitters."

For Gullickson, making it to the NLDS was quite an accomplishment. Many players never make it to post-season play, but Gullickson did in his second full season — or half a season if you consider 1981 was a strike-shortened campaign. He had been selected by the Expos in the 1977 June draft, the same one that produced future teammates Tim Raines and Scott Sanderson.

Gullickson had been 10–5 in 1980 with a nifty 3.00 ERA and his stellar season had included an 18-strikeout performance. Getting diagnosed with type 1 diabetes at spring training in 1980 had not been a deterrent; it was one of the few times in Expos history that a player was diagnosed with a major disease.

"With or without diabetes, I would have been in the majors," he said.

"It was discovered in our spring training physicals within the first two days," recalled Expos trainer Ron McClain. "It was certainly the first major thing we found. It was unusual to detect diabetes in a 21-year-old. We had a sandwich for him to eat during games as he expended energy while pitching. We helped monitor his blood sugar. We kept a current vial of insulin available. We kept glucose tablets for him in case his sugar went too low. But he was generally quite versed in his diabetic care and did probably 98 percent of it himself."

So with Rogers and Gullickson shutting down the Phillies in the first two games, all of a sudden the Expos were up 2–0 in the best-of-five set as the series switched to Philadelphia. It would turn out to be far from easy

ROGERS ALL BUSINESS DECLINING WIFE'S IDEA

The Expos checked in late in Philadelphia after Game 2 of the NLDS and Steve Rogers and his wife went to bed for a good sleep.

The next day, Robin brought up an idea.

"Hey, what are we going to do?" she asked her husband.

"We're not going to do anything," he replied. "I'm not mad or upset but I'm here to pitch the fifth game of the series."

Rogers's wife had wondered if they might go out on the town, go for a fancy dinner and catch a movie or play or something like that. The pitcher would have none of it. There might not even be a fifth game, but if there was he would be the starting pitcher.

So there was Rogers putting full concentration on the series, even with the Expos enjoying a 2–0 lead in games. Going out on the town would be a distraction.

"I'm here to do one thing," he told his wife. "I'm here to pitch the fifth game, if needed. I am going to throw a shutout. Every single pitch is important."

Rogers was in Philly to win the series, even if he had to wait until the fifth game, which he did. Distractions had to go.

"Don't let yourself relax," he was saying to himself, and his wife understood. "She got it. There was no disappointment."

in the City of Brotherly Love. Philadelphia fans are known to jeer not only the opposition but even their own players, so going into Philadelphia and trying to win was not going to be a cakewalk.

It was a far different story in Game 3, which was played without an off-day following Game 2. The Phillies won 6–2, but Fanning played the game under protest after an Expos triple play was negated. With help from retrosheet.org, here's how that play developed.

On a bunt popped up by pitcher Larry Christenson, Expos catcher Gary Carter appeared to catch the ball on the fly, but there was no call from home-plate umpire Bruce Froemming. Carter, figuring if Christenson wasn't out on the fly the force must be on, threw to Larry Parrish at third and third-base umpire Jerry Crawford signalled "Out!" That's one. But, umpire Crawford later explained, he meant "out" on the *batter.* He thought Carter had made the catch. But that explanation was in the future. In the live action, Parrish then whipped it to Warren Cromartie at first, before Christenson got there. That's two. Larry Bowa by now had left second, so Expos second-baseman Jerry Manuel got the ball, ran up, and tripled Bowa off. That's three. Second-base umpire John Kibler seemed to call Bowa out but then said he had called "Time" before the out. After an umpires' huddle, the triple play was upheld — and then it was negated by National League president Chub Feeney, who was in the crowd watching the game. This all caused a 10-minute delay and, at the end of it, Fanning played the game under protest.

But, really, on-again-off-again triple play or not, the Expos were done in by the Phillies' bats, stellar six-inning work by Christenson, and a nifty double play turned by Mike Schmidt, who speared a line drive by Manuel, prompting backup Expos player Mike Phillips to say, "That's the best play I ever saw a third-baseman make."

Game 4 was a tight battle won by the Phillies 6–5, thanks to a ninth-inning pinch-hit home run off of Reardon by rarely used puppy George Vukovich. The Expos had rallied from a 4–0 deficit to shake things up. Vukovich had been wonderful during the regular season in a part-time role, going 10-for-26. Against the Expos in the playoffs, he never cooled off, going 4-for-9. He was ultra-hot. Vukovich had made his major-league debut with the Phillies in 1980, appearing as a pinch-hitter in a game against the Expos. He even received a 1980 World Series ring, although he did not play in the final series itself.

Vukovich stepped in against Reardon and lined a shot over the right-field fence, going down near his ankles to get Reardon's pitch, which the reliever said at the time was "down and in and right where I wanted it." By that time, Reardon was into his third inning of relief. In video and still photos from the game, Reardon can be seen on the bench with his head in his hands as the Phillies celebrated. "I remember the home run," Reardon said in 2017. "I felt bad. Back then, closers threw two or three innings." And so, it came to a showdown — the fifth and deciding game.

Years later, Expos majority owner Charles Bronfman would get up close and personal with reporter Nancy Southam of *Southam News* following the Expos' loss to the Phillies in Game 4, a setback that forced the fifth and deciding game.

"I couldn't breathe anymore," Bronfman told Southam. "I sat there destroyed. I had a debate within myself, whether I could handle another game."

He did. And the Expos would win the fifth game.

Chapter 13

An Unexpected
Pre-Game Pep Talk

There was a bit of gloom and doom as Warren Cromartie, Andre Dawson, Jerry White, and Jerry Manuel sat down for Sunday breakfast the morning of Game 5.

After the Phillies had come back from a 2–0 deficit to force Game 5, with the help of George Vukovich's walk-off homer off of Jeff Reardon in Game 4, "We all looked kind of gloomy," Cromartie remembered.

Gloomy because the Phillies were the defending World Series champions and were tough at home. Gloomy because crafty southpaw Steve Carlton would be on the mound for the Phillies to face Expos veteran Steve Rogers. Rogers and the Expos had already beaten Carlton once in the series, but to beat Carlton a second time was very much a tall order.

As the quartet of Expos chatted, they got the surprise of their life when a six-foot-nine man walked over. They all craned their necks to look *waaay* up. It was Boston Celtics legend Bill Russell, one of the greatest players in NBA history. The gloom and doom was soon replaced by cheer.

"It was the day of the game we had to win. Bill was in there eating," Cromartie said. "He stopped over to see us. It was a real surprise to see him. We were having breakfast and he walked over. We met him. I don't know why he was there. He gave us a pep talk. We were glad that he was there. We were all in awe when he came over to the table. We all wanted to say hello. He saw the gloominess in our eyes and that maybe we didn't give ourselves enough of a chance and that we didn't give ourselves enough credit."

So what did Russell do? He gave the Four Wise Men a little picker-upper. With Russell realizing that the Expos were up against a vaunted opponent in the Phillies, especially with them playing in their own backyard, a hostile environment for Montreal, he offered some advice.

"Just give your best. Nothing is impossible. Don't be afraid. Anything can happen. Go at it. Have some fun. Beat the best," Russell told the four.

"It was a real motivational type of speech, very inspirational," Cromartie said. "It was quite a blessing. It was good timing for us. He doesn't have enough fingers for all of his rings. He was the real, true champion."

That's right, he has eight fingers and two thumbs, but he has 11 rings after helping the Celtics win 11 NBA championships during his 13-season career. Better believe it that the four Expos were in awe of Russell, even though he had been out of the game as a player for a dozen years. He had retired in 1969, the same year the Expos began operations as an expansion team. Russell is widely considered one of the best players in NBA history, along with the likes of Michael Jordan, Oscar Robertson, LeBron James, and Kobe Bryant. There was Russell's scoring ability, his shot-blocking prowess, his suffocating man-to-man defence.

There weren't many better than Russell from 1956 to 1969. He was the Celtics' pacemaker. He had helped steer the University of San Francisco to two NCAA titles and he was a member of the 1956 gold-medal-winning U.S. Olympic basketball squad.

"His talk with us was very encouraging. He gave us the confidence to do things," Cromartie said.

"We all ate together at times for breakfast, and to remember a tall figure like Bill coming through and giving words of encouragement was really something," White said.

A few hours later, Rogers out-duelled Carlton in another epic matchup and the Expos won 3–0. For the second time in the series, Rogers had gone toe-to-toe with Carlton and won. Two of the most uplifting efforts made by Rogers in his brilliant career.

Carlton's 0–2 record in the series is misleading. For one thing, Game 5 didn't start that good for the Expos because Carlton struck out Cromartie, White, and Dawson in the first inning.

But Rogers did it all on the mound and at the plate that day. He pitched a complete game and delivered a bonus: a two-run single to centre with the bases loaded and two out in the fifth. Larry Parrish cashed in the other Montreal run with an RBI double in the sixth after Dawson had led off with a single.

Rogers even had another single, while shutting down the Phillies on six hits. George Vukovich, the Phillies' hero of Game 4, made the starting lineup for the game, but Rogers struck him out twice and handed him an 0-for-4 outing. In the bottom of the ninth, the Phillies hit the ball hard, but all for three outs. Mike Schmidt lined to Dawson in centre, Gary Matthews roped one to Terry Francona in left, and Manny Trillo

Warren Cromartie has all the attention to himself after catching the last out of NLDS vs. Phillies.

scorched one a few inches above the head and into the glove of Cromartie at first. Cromartie snagged the ball and ran as fast as he could with his ball and glove high above his head to mob Rogers with his teammates.

"It was not a surprise to see what Steve did against the Phillies. He was on his game. He just went out and dominated Carlton," Expos pitching coach Galen Cisco said.

Phillies star third-baseman Mike Schmidt could only praise Rogers. "They outplayed us and Rogers outpitched us and even outhit us. My hat's off to Steve Rogers," Schmidt said.

"It was a tremendous series. The Expos had great pitching from Steve Rogers and timely hitting," Dave Van Horne said. "In two games, Steve was up against a future Hall of Famer in Steve Carlton and came out on top in both. It was the culmination of a great run by Steve. In that Philadelphia series, he was wonderful against a very good team."

Within a few seconds of nabbing the final out, Cromartie spotted someone with a Canadian flag. "I saw someone with a Canadian flag. These guys walked over and gave it to me," Cromartie said. "That was a moment of joy. We had come off the field and a couple of the guys were calling me over. I saw the flag and I grabbed it and started waving it."

As someone who had played both in Quebec City and Montreal, Cromartie knew the symbolism of his act.

"This is Canada's moment. It was a very proud moment. I had played in Montreal and I played in Quebec City. I married a girl from Quebec City. The flag had a big impact on Canada. Put it this way: it put a little cherry on the banana split. It was talked about all over Canada and it still does [have an impact] to this day."

Cromartie identified the duo with the flag as twin brothers by the name of Gorman. Before he was finished, Cromartie headed toward the Phillies' dugout to wave the flag — a little nudge in the ribs for the Phillies players. He then "gave the flag back to the twins," he said. Twenty years later, the legendary image still lived on in Montreal. On the 20th anniversary of the event, the twins and Cromartie were featured in person in the Montreal studio of TSN 690 talk-show legend Mitch Melnick.

"What Warren [Cromartie] did was an awesome gesture, very spontaneous," Rogers remembered. "It should be one of those moments that

Canadian baseball fans should honestly always remember. Carrying that flag was very symbolic."

Sitting in the stands for Game 5 in Philadelphia was Expos majority-owner Charles Bronfman, a nervous wreck as he watched his team. He said his "heart was beating very hard."

Away from the field, Bronfman and his brother Edgar had days earlier completed a huge business deal — purchasing almost 25 percent of the chemical giant Du Pont, after Du Pont had outbid Seagram for the oil giant Conoco months earlier.

"We had just become the largest shareholder of Du Pont," Bronfman remembered. "And Ed Jefferson, the CEO of Du Pont, was at the deciding game in Philadelphia, sitting right behind me. At one point in the game, I turned around to him and said, 'Jeff, compared to this, Du Pont was a cinch!'"

As the players headed off the field to taste the Mumm's Cordon Rouge 1976, Steve Rogers stopped by the media room for interviews. National League official Blake Cullen helped get the questions rolling and had the misfortune of pissing Rogers off royally. Clearly, Cullen got under Rogers's skin by asking him to talk "about the rap that you can't win the big ones." Rogers just looked at Cullen and snapped, "Next question, please."

When we talked in 2016 about the game, Rogers said, "I remember that I was [as] on as I had ever been. I was so locked in. My sinker was a really heavy, heavy ball. I was throwing my breaking ball for strikes. In the top of the eighth, we're up 3–0, and all of a sudden, the strike zone just disappeared. I remember Larry Parrish walking in from third and saying, 'The umpire is screwing you.' I remember I had to calm down Larry."

It was a scenario that Parrish couldn't remember, but we asked Parrish about Rogers, and this is what he had to say: "Steve was a great pitcher for the Expos and for whatever reason, he was … maligned for not being able to win the big game, and for him to step up on the playoff stage and face Carlton and win two games was quite something.

"I remember watching old film of Pete Rose and an interview he did about 1975 when Cincinnati played Boston in the World Series. Rose talked about how much fun he was having, about the competition between the two clubs. Some players would be nervous about the outcome but Rose was just enjoying the competition. I think if you could take that approach, it would be a whole lot easier to perform, instead of worrying about the negative things that might happen."

After beating the Phillies, it was on to Los Angeles for the NLCS. It just so happened that the same day the Expos won, the Dodgers ousted the Houston Astros 3–2 in the other best-of-five NLDS. The Dodgers had lost the first two games before roaring back to win three straight.

"I remember we took a charter flight with Air Canada from Philadelphia to Los Angeles on the Canadian Thanksgiving weekend. I thought it would be pretty wild, but it was subdued," assistant trainer Mike Kozak reminisced in 2017.

That's right. As Expos pitcher Ray Burris said years later, "We still had business to do."

And Rogers had the game ball from Game 5 against the Phillies to cherish on the trip out west. Cromartie had given it to him after the game but he lost it, and he shrieked in the clubhouse before getting a clubhouse attendant to look for it.

Sure enough, the ball was found in Rogers's duffel bag and to this day, it's a treasured piece of memorabilia for Rogers, especially since he batted and pitched the Expos to the win.

"It is in a box along with my shutout ball, All-Star Game balls, and team balls," Rogers told me. "I just saw my Expos team ball from 1973 while my five siblings and I divided the personal items of our parents' estate. It's funny I knew it was from '73 before I even saw a name, because it was a horsehide ball and '73 was the last year of horsehide. They went to cowhide in 1974."

Part Four

THE NATIONAL LEAGUE CHAMPIONSHIP SERIES

Chapter 14

Dodgers Take Game 1

O
ne hurdle removed, one looming. The Phillies were eliminated, and now the Dodgers were ripe for the taking.

On the day off, or off-day, as they say in baseball lingo, the Expos' October 3 hero Wallace Johnson was dropped from the roster for the NLCS against the Dodgers and the injured Rodney Scott was put back in.

Scott would replace Jerry Manuel at second, and as it turned out, would play the entire series against the Dodgers (Manuel had gone 1-for-14 in the Phillies series). Johnson was also a second-baseman, but the Expos' brain trust decided to go with experience in Scott, who had started his big-league career in 1975 with the Kansas City Royals.

Scott had ended up with the Expos for a few games in 1976, but played for Oakland in 1977 and the Cubs in 1978 before finding his way back to Montreal in a trade following the '78 season.

More importantly, Tim Raines was healthy again, allowing him to swing the bat and play left field. Raines had been kept on the ros-ter for the NLDS against the Phillies despite the broken hand, but for pinch-running only.

Expos GM John McHale also dropped pitcher Tom Gorman for the Dodgers series and reactivated outfielder Rowland Office, who had been trying to get back on track since the Ellis Valentine throw from the outfield.

The Expos had a late-afternoon practice to unwind a bit and celebrate their win over the Phillies. Likewise, the Dodgers seized the chance to rest up a bit after eliminating the Houston Astros 3–2 in their series.

On the day of the series opener, a *Los Angeles Times* headline read "Team Canada vs. Team L.A."

Expos sophomore Bill Gullickson was up against cagey veteran Burt Hooton of the Dodgers in the first game, and the young pitcher impressed in his third post-season career start after winning one and losing one to the Phillies.

The Dodgers took an early 2–0 lead in the second inning. It all got started when Steve Garvey singled and Ron Cey doubled him home. Mike Scioscia singled to centre, moving Cey to third. Cey then scored on Bill Russell's sacrifice bunt.

Hooton's quirky knuckle curveball kept Expos bats off balance for most of the game and he got extra protection in the eighth inning when Montreal closer Jeff Reardon came into the game. It was a debatable, peculiar move by manager Jim Fanning, considering that the Expos were down 2–0 and it was not a save opportunity. There were other capable pitchers in the bullpen, such as Scott Sanderson, Elias Sosa, Woodie Fryman, and Bill Lee, but it was easy to see that in tight situations in this final series that Fanning was going to go with a core group of four pitchers: Rogers, Gullickson, Burris, and Reardon.

Reardon admitted to me that he actually asked Fanning if he could pitch in that situation.

"Back then, closers wanted to stay sharp and get work," Reardon said. "I needed some work."

Reardon retired the first two batters, but Cey singled and then Pedro Guerrero and Scioscia both homered. Instead of being in a tight game, the Dodgers were now up 5–0. It would be the last time Reardon would pitch in the post-season in 1981.

In the top of the ninth, the Expos did mount a little rally. Bob Welch, who had relieved Hooton in the eighth inning, was out to start the ninth and promptly gave up consecutive doubles to Gary Carter and Larry Parrish. At that point, with the Expos scoring a run, Welch was replaced by Steve Howe. Cromartie promptly greeted Howe with a single and Parrish went to third. But Howe got Jerry White to pop up and Chris Speier hit into a double play, one of four double plays the Dodgers turned in the game.

Game 1 went to the Dodgers, 5–1.

Chapter 15

Game 2: Ray Burris Slighted, Pitches Masterpiece

G ame 1 of the NLCS was over at Chavez Ravine, and Ray Burris found his way back to the historic Biltmore Hotel in downtown Los Angeles, where the Expos were staying.

Burris quickly turned on the television and found a local NBC sports announcer rhyming off the names of the starting lineup for Game 2 the next day.

"The broadcaster was going through the lineups for each club," Burris told me in mid-2017. "He mentioned every name of the Dodgers and every name of the Expos, except that he didn't announce mine. Wow!

"The lineups were in bright, bold letters. He never mentioned my name. I was really ticked off. I had a hard time with that disrespect. I remember the motivation — I was really motivated. I was going out to compete against the baseball world and the media. The writers out there felt the Dodgers were going up 2–0 in the series."

But, hey, hold that. Burris would have nothing to do with the disrespect he was getting, so he went out and pitched one of the best games of his life, of his career. The veteran of nine seasons was on a mission at Dodger Stadium. He shut up the Dodgers, the Los Angeles media, and especially the broadcaster who had failed to mention his name the night before.

Burris went the distance, out-duelling rookie sensation Fernando Valenzuela. Final score: Expos 3, Dodgers 0. It was an achievement of the highest degree. The Expos' fortunes at Dodger Stadium had been pitiful prior to this. Going back to 1978, the Expos were 1–19 in Los Angeles. As Burris recalled,

> Not to take anything away from Fernando Valenzuela, I was quite capable myself as a pitcher. I had more years in baseball than him. I wanted to display my talents. Valenzuela could be beat. It wasn't the best game of my career, but it was the best game of mine in the post-season. It was pretty phenomenal to tie the series going back to Montreal.
>
> I wanted the opportunity to get in front of the podium in the media room after the game. I told the media, "Ladies and gentlemen, thank you for coming out to see our ballclub. We've got a top-notch club." I explained to them right then what happened with the announcer. I never got an apology. I was penalized. They never asked for an interview, and I wasn't going to let them, no. Absolutely. I told them there would be no questions, and I told them, "Have a good evening." I told them point-blank.
>
> The individual media was not to blame. It was the big giant NBC. They had no courtesy or respect to announce my name on the broadcast.

As he left the media room chock full of many national writers, Burris ran into advance scout Charlie Fox and gave him a hug. Fox had scouted the Dodgers/Astros NLDS and had suggested to Burris that the Dodgers' largely right-handed hitting lineup might be vulnerable to off-speed breaking balls, so Burris took him up on it and shut the Dodgers down on five hits. Burris may have declined to take questions from the national media in the official interview room, but on the side, later, to one Montreal writer, Burris opined this way: "The people came out to see Valenzuela, but they found a new star."

Even the Los Angeles writers were scratching their heads at what Burris had done.

"Losing to Ray Burris was to the Dodgers a surprise on the order of the Little Big Horn," wrote Mark Heisler, the Dodgers' beat scribe for the *Los Angeles Times*. "Burris is an ex-Cub, an ex-Met, and an ex-Yankee, all in the last three seasons. The Dodgers had their hearts set on taking the 2–0 lead, which was going to give Jerry Reuss a chance at the knockout on Friday followed by a three-day rest for everyone before the World Series. Now, it's going back to their frozen turf for its conclusion."

The legendary *Times* play-on-words maestro Jim Murray said: "Arrayed against him [Valenzuela] was a migrant worker named Ray Burris, one of those pitchers who has been through more towns than a steamboat trunk."

Even Jay Johnstone of the Dodgers took a shot at Burris: "Every dog has his day. What's his record in the National League?"

Then an unidentified Dodger, according to Heisler's game story, said: "Let me put it this way: if I had $5,000 handy, I'd have bet $5,000 we'd beat him."

Like the NBC broadcaster, most people were giving Burris the Rodney Dangerfield handle, but he sure shoved it down the Dodgers' throats.

Burris had had to wait until February 18, just a few days before spring training, to get a contract in 1981. He had offers from other teams, but Expos GM John McHale finally ponied up the most cash: $325,000 — not bad coin in those days. McHale had actually tried to persuade another free agent, Don Sutton, to come to Montreal. McHale even offered Sutton a three-year contract and owner Charles Bronfman convinced Sutton to meet him at a private airport near Montreal.

But Sutton declined the Expos' offer, muttering to Bronfman about the extra tax penalty of playing in Canada and the hassles of going through customs and immigration.

Burris made McHale's gamble pay off grandly and as much as he was peeved with the NBC broadcaster, he was able to smile a little when he told a *Times* reporter that in the middle of the game, he was getting hungry. Not just hungry to shut down the Dodgers, but hungry for food. He said he would have liked a cheeseburger.

"I wish I'd had one," Burris said, smiling. "It might have put an extra five miles an hour on my fastball."

BEFORE SKYPE, SUTHERLAND TUNED IN TO THE EXPOS ANY WAY POSSIBLE

Canadian-born actor Donald Sutherland was one of the Expos' most diehard fans over the years, especially in 1981 — so much so that he did his darndest to listen in or see every game possible, even with technical assistance.

"This was long before Skype and Donald was in France and he would have somebody in the U.S. hook him up long distance with a phone receiver next to a radio," recalled 1981 Expos call-up Dan Briggs. "He was a real fan. I don't know why but he was. He loved Montreal. He'd sit right next to our dugout. When I didn't play, I got talking to Donald. One game, we invited him into the clubhouse. He had a good time."

During one stretch late in the 1981 season and in the playoffs, Sutherland apparently never missed a game either on the road or at the Big O. He had at least one superstition, telling writer Brodie Snyder that year, "I'm afraid to change clothes."

Said Parrish: "I can remember Donald coming to almost all of the games. He was at our games in Montreal often. This is a guy who was at the height of his career. He would still sit right in the stadium, right among the people, not in a box above but close to the dugout. It was a time when it was sort of popular to be an Expo.

"He was a great actor. I told him I really liked his character Oddball in the movie *Kelly's Heroes*."

I reached out to Sutherland for this book, but his publicist said he was too busy, shooting two productions back-to-back.

Born in Saint John, New Brunswick, he spent his teen years in Bridgewater, Nova Scotia. He has a summer home in the tourist town of Georgeville, Quebec, in the Eastern Townships near Montreal.

Burris had advanced from relative obscurity, rising from Idabel, a small town in Oklahoma, to make it to the major leagues after getting noticed first at nearby Duke High School.

As a boy, Burris grew up idolizing St. Louis Cardinals icon Bob Gibson and gave notice to the baseball world with eye-catching seasons of

15–10, 15–13, and 14–16 with the Chicago Cubs, who selected him in the 17th round of the 1972 amateur draft out of little-known Southwestern Oklahoma State University, located in the equally inconspicuous community of Weatherford. He is believed to be the only Bulldogs alumni baseball player to ever make it to the big leagues. Pretty impressive.

"I was 16–4 as a junior in college and that really helped me get my name on the radar," Burris said. "It wasn't how high I got drafted. I think the opportunity to get into the NAIA World Series in Phoenix in 1971 really helped me. It was just an opportunity to get a chance. I'm thankful for the Cubs to give me a chance in the draft."

By the late 1970s, Burris's time in the limelight was fading. In 1979, he threw for the Cubs, Yankees, and Mets. With the Yankees, he was used strictly as a reliever. He spent the entire 1980 season with the Mets, with lacklustre results: he was 7–13. But McHale saw something in him and decided to sign him.

"Ray Burris pitched some great games for us," pitching coach Galen Cisco remembered. "He was one of those guys who wanted to do good. He had a so-so year prior to that [1980] but he was very conscientious and bought into our program. [He] and I worked hard, getting his game straightened out."

McHale decided to take the advice of club scout Eddie Lopat, who said this about Burris at spring training in 1981: "In the last year or so, he has become a pitcher."

In Game 2, Burris kept the Dodgers off balance with a lot of breaking stuff rather than showing them too much of his fastball. But the Expos didn't get off on the right foot that night. Tim Raines singled to start the game but was quickly caught off first by Valenzuela and thrown out at second in a rundown between first-baseman Steve Garvey and shortstop Bill Russell.

Raines made up for his miscue by drilling an RBI single in the fourth after Warren Cromartie had doubled home a run. In the sixth, with Valenzuela out of the game, Andre Dawson singled to right and scored when Dodgers left-fielder Dusty Baker muffed a base hit by Gary Carter.

"The rains in Spain may stay mostly in the plains. In Montreal, the Raines goes all over the place. It never Raines but it scores. Raines drops kept falling on [the Dodgers'] heads," Jim Murray mused in the *Times* about Raines, who went 3-for-5.

On the final play of the game, Burris got Baker to line into a 6–4 double play. Baker scorched the ball into the hole between short and third, but shortstop Chris Speier ranged to his right and snared the ball at his shoelaces. He then threw to second-baseman Rodney Scott to double up Steve Garvey, setting up a mini-whoop-up of Expos players. Instead of the traditional handshakes that take place following most games, hugging, backslapping, and hand-slapping was the norm as the Expos celebrated the huge win at Dodger Stadium.

"The Expos held an impromptu celebration on the field and the series began the transition into its Arctic phase," *Times* beat reporter Mark Heisler wrote.

Yes, cold and all, the series was going to Montreal tied 1–1.

"It was 60 degrees [15°C] today in Montreal," manager Jim Fanning was telling reporters at Dodger Stadium. "That's an awfully nice fall day for us. Whatever the weather will be will be right for us. We will live with it. Part of being a Montreal player is playing in April and September. It's nice to be playing in October. We use hand-warmers, heavy coats, heavy gloves, heaters, anything to keep warm."

Just the kind of scenario the players from Hollywood weren't familiar with.

"I remember the feeling, the very confident feeling we had coming home to Montreal," Wallace Johnson remembered. "We were very confident that we could finish them off in Montreal. Nobody from southern California likes to play in cold Montreal. They had to come to the cold north."

Chapter 16

In Montreal: Dodgers Hate "The Happy Wanderer"

Yes, the cold would be a distraction for the Dodgers when they arrived at Olympic Stadium on the afternoon of October 15.

Not only the cold, but also the song "The Happy Wanderer."

It used to drive Dodgers players — and players on other teams — crazy when they came to Montreal and heard organist Fern Lapierre start playing "The Happy Wanderer" and thousands of Expos fans starting to sing their motivational song.

"Between Youppi! and the song … !" Dodgers left fielder Dusty Baker said to me in 2017, with a smile on his face and shaking his head.

"It's not meant to be a disrespectful thing. Montreal is a lovely town, but every time you go there, over and over, they would play 'The Happy Wanderer,'" Rick Monday said, also shaking his head. "*Val-deri, val-dera … !*"

It was no different prior to and during the third game of the NLCS with the best-of-five affair tied 1–1. The song was playing again.

"'The Happy Wanderer' song was a long-time favourite. Fern started playing it at Jarry Park, and the fans always joined in singing," recalled Expos scoreboard operator Paul Shubin.

"THE HAPPY WANDERER"

I love to go a-wandering along the mountain track
And as I go I love to sing, my knapsack on my back
Val-deri, val-dera, val-deri, val-dera-ha-ha-ha-ha-ha
Val-deri, val-dera, my knapsack on my back
I love to wander by the stream that dances in the sun
So joyously it calls to me "Come join my happy song"
Val-deri, val-dera, vald-eri, val-dera-ha-ha-ha-ha-ha
Val-deri, val-dera, come join my happy song
I wave my hat to all I meet and they wave back to me
And blackbirds call so loud and sweet from every green wood tree
Val-deri, val-dera, val-deri, val-dera-ha-ha-ha-ha-ha
Val-deri, val-dera, from every greenwood tree
High overhead the skylarks wing, they never rest at home
But just like me they love to sing as o'er the world we roam
Val-deri, val-dera, val-deri, valdera-ha-ha-ha-ha-ha
Val-deri, val-dera, as o'er the world we roam
O may I go a-wandering until the day I die
And may I always laugh and sing beneath God's clear blue sky
Val-deri, val-dera, val-deri val-dera-ha-ha-ha-ha-ha
Val-deri, val-dera, beneath God's clear blue sky
    — Original composition by Florenz Friedrich Sigismund
        (1788–1857), "Mein Vater war ein Wandersmann"

"That song would get on your nerves," recalled Mark Cresse, who was a coach for the Dodgers from 1974 to 1988.

The lyrics were written in German by Florenz Friedrich Sigismund (1788–1857), but the song's popularity wasn't realized until the twentieth century, almost 100 years after he died, when Friedrich-Wilhelm Möller modernized it.

In turn, Möller's sister Edith adapted the song for her Obernkirchen Children's Choir. The song received widespread attention when the BBC broadcast the choir's winning performance at the Llangollen International Musical Eisteddfod, and it turned into an international hit.

If the song wasn't enough to drive the Dodgers bonkers before Game 3, there was also the cold, the pre-game introductions, and a decision made by their manager, Tommy Lasorda.

Monday recalled that all of the pre-game introductions were a distraction. But so was Lasorda's decision not to let his players wear jackets while the introductions were being made.

"Tommy was trying to say that the worst thing to do is read the newspapers in the opposing city, but it's impossible not to read the papers," Monday said. "Tommy was telling us that guys from Hollywood, nobody wears jackets. We'll see how tough we are. It's obviously colder in Montreal in October than it is in Los Angeles, and they had no roof.

"So we're standing on the third-base line and they were introducing all of the Expos, their locker-room personnel, the dignitaries from Montreal. It's a wonder they didn't introduce the entire stadium. And we're not wearing jackets. It's the elements. Tommy, in his infinite wisdom, said we wouldn't wear jackets."

Chapter 17

Game 3: Jerry White Hits Big Homer

J erry White did a quasi–Carlton Fisk backward run, minus the waving-fair move, if only for a second. Then he spun around and ran forward. He had hit a home run.

Unlike Fisk, frantically waving the ball to be fair in the 1975 World Series, White knew his smash was fair — the biggest home run ever hit by an Expo in the team's 36-season history.

White's at-bat was a battle of the Jerrys: Jerry White and Dodgers pitcher Jerry Reuss. The Dodgers and Expos were tied 1–1 in the bottom of the sixth inning. The best-of-five series was tied 1–1 after the split at Chavez Ravine.

Mike Scioscia's RBI groundout in the fourth inning against Steve Rogers had given the Dodgers a 1–0 lead and Reuss was coasting along until the Expos' half of the sixth. Reuss retired the first two Montreal batters, with Tim Raines grounding out 5–3 and Rodney Scott popping up to second. But there was trouble ahead. Next up was Andre Dawson, who singled to left, then Gary Carter walked, and Larry Parrish delivered a run-scoring single to tie the game.

That brought switch-hitter White to the plate, batting right-handed against southpaw Reuss. There was White, the super sub, famous as the

A drive to left field. Home run. Jerry White, a three-run homer for the Expos. Jerry White tees off. He knew it had a chance. There it is. A 4–1 lead for the Expos in the sixth inning. The left fielder didn't have a chance. At Olympic Stadium, the most vocal, enthusiastic crowd we've ever seen witness a baseball game is ecstatic.

— Expos play-by-play voice Dave Van Horne describing Jerry White's home run, October 16, 1981 (Permission: MLB Productions)

club's fourth outfielder and last remaining member of the Expos' BUS squad, the group of part-time players formed years earlier by Tommy Hutton, who had recently been released.

Reuss came inside on White and White pulled it, just to the right of the foul-pole screen and into the left-field seats. That gave the Expos a go-ahead 4–1 lead, which they held on to. The Expos now had a 2–1 lead in the best-of-five NLCS.

"Jerry Reuss was very tough," White said. "He had that hard cutter that came into you. That was my third at-bat against him that game. I just got into the pitch more than I thought. I hit it pretty good. I don't think he

Jerry White hits a home run off of Jerry Reuss with Ron Cey looking on.

made a mistake. It's just that the ball didn't come in as much. For a little guy to hit that home run was special."

It was so special that a deafening crowd of 54,372 cheered as he rounded the bases and hit the dugout. After the game, his teammates laid out a red carpet to his stall in the clubhouse. Very touching.

"I vaguely remember that. Wow!" White said after I reminded him about the carpet treatment.

Reuss doesn't remember that the Dodgers had any scouting reports on White. Reuss told me, chuckling,

> Our scouting reports back then weren't that detailed. It consisted of Tommy Lasorda standing in front of the club and talking about no one in particular, "He's a better high-ball hitter. Keep the ball down and mix it up."
>
> Once, in a pre-game meeting, Tommy stated the batter was "a good first-ball fastball hitter," which prompted Burt Hooton, a pitcher sitting next to me, to ask me quietly, "Does that mean we throw a bad fastball on the first pitch?"
>
> As far as Jerry's scouting report, I don't remember. Since I crowded most right-handed batters anyway, I did pitch him on the inside part of the plate. It seemed to work as Jerry got three hits in 17 at-bats against me during the regular season. He put the ball in play, as I never walked him and he struck out just once.

Teammates and friends didn't call White "Hit Man" for nothing. He had different aliases. Some people called him Jerome, which is his given first name. Some people called him Reggie, after Reggie Smith of the Dodgers, because both sported Afro hairstyles.

"People thought I was a smaller version of Reggie," White said.

Following the game, White faced a barrage of reporters from both Canada and the U.S. and mentioned that another nickname had been bestowed upon him. "They kid me about my power," White told the scribes. "The guys call me the Toy Cannon. I don't know what it is when I hit an important home run. It just happens."

Jerry White is all smiles after his Game 3 home run in this collage of photos.

"That home run against Jerry Reuss was good for Canadians," White told me in 2017. "I was a hero then, a goat later on. I'm trying to be professional. Nobody is perfect. If you fail, you get hard on yourself. I had too good a career playing and coaching to let go, though."

Without a doubt, it was one of the most significant home runs ever hit on Canadian soil.

"Yes, I'm really proud of that honour, but if I ever did something almost as great in the game, it would be satisfying," White said. "Sometimes, it's the little things that are exciting, like getting the runners over to second and third with a sacrifice bunt that helps win a game. That's exciting, too."

As we get back to that home run off of Reuss, the obvious question to ask is this: Is that the most satisfying home run of White's career? Oddly, the answer is no.

> The biggest thrill, you know what it is? The home run in San Francisco against Vida Blue in the 1970s. I grew up in the San Francisco area, cheering everything Giants. I was always there at the Giants games with my Giants uniform. At that time, you could stand behind the players at the fence because they were standing-room only seats from Christopher Milk coupons that cost 50 cents and you were in.

> The game I hit the home run against Vida Blue, all my family and friends were there and I hit third in the lineup and played centre field just like Willie Mays did, and what a game I had in front of all who attended.

White doesn't know the date or year he hit the home run off of Blue but he thought it might have been the late 1970s.

White also remembers another home run that had its hilarious undertones. White was playing for St. Louis against the Dodgers in 1986 and hit a home run off of Tom Niedenfuer.

But what happened in the moments leading up to the dinger caused White to crack up.

Dodgers manager Tommy Lasorda, who obviously remembered White's heroics in the 1981 NLCS, told Dodgers catcher Alex Trevino to get Niedenfuer to throw White certain pitches. But White had a secret weapon.

> It was the bottom of the 12th inning. I was pinch-hitting. Whitey Herzog was the St. Louis manager. Tommy Lasorda was calling pitches. Him and Trevino spoke Spanish. And I spoke and understood Spanish. I learned Spanish in Mexico in 1974. My kids are Spanish. I played winter ball in Venezuela in 1978–79.
>
> Niedenfuer was trying to close out the game. Lasorda was saying to Trevino in Spanish that Tom should throw the ball outside. I picked up what they were saying. They didn't know I spoke and understood Spanish. I didn't swing at the first pitch. I wanted to get a feel for the velocity of the ball. The next pitch, it might have been a strike. I didn't swing. Then they said to throw me a ball outside.
>
> I was waiting for the next pitch and hit the ball out of the park at old Busch Stadium to tie the game. The Dodgers won in the 13th inning.
>
> I've never seen Tommy to get a chance to tell him the story.

Then there was White's inside-the-park home run off Bob Forsch of the Cardinals, one that also had its undercurrents.

> The home run off of Forsch was a curveball. He had a very deliberate windup and it was easy to see the ball. But anyway, the night before the game, I was packing my bags, cleaning the apartment, and washing dishes and I cut my left ring finger. Off to the emergency room I went to get two or three stitches about 3:30 that morning, so you could imagine what was going through my head.
>
> That morning we left, I explained to the Expos what happened and they thought I had gotten into a fight, which really cracks me up to this day. But anyway, long story short, my finger was all wrapped up with gauze that day or night we started and I got by that day and was able to play. So the home run was extra special even if I was bandaged up.

Steve Rogers's Game 3 effort against the Dodgers was his third win of the post-season, cementing his reputation as the best pitcher in Expos history.

"Steve was as good as I'd ever seen him," Reuss said.

"I didn't have my good stuff," Rogers admitted. "Only my sinker was really working."

Whatever the truth is, the win left the Expos one game short of the World Series. The night before White homered, the New York Yankees had polished off the Oakland Athletics three straight to win the American League championship and a berth in the World Series, which would start in New York a few days later. The game in Montreal had fans in that city, the province of Quebec, and the country of Canada excited about what might lie ahead.

"It's a national thing," Rogers told reporters following the Game 3 victory. "We have national TV and we're seen across Canada. I guess we're the best show in town right now."

Chapter 18

Game 4: Dodgers
Tie the Series

I can tell you we were packed and ready to go to the World Series for three consecutive days. Seeing we were in the playoffs, Jim Fanning said the bat boys were going on all of the road trips. Jim said we would be part of the travel with the team. We had to have our luggage packed and ready for the game because we were going to leave after the game.

— 1981 Expos bat boy Frank Albertson

All the Expos had to do was win another game and they were off to the Big Apple. During Game 4, an Air Canada jet sat on the tarmac at Dorval Airport ready to take the team on to New York. There were 54,499 fans in the stands, most of them expecting a win.

After they lost on Jerry White's home run in Game 3, the Dodgers backtracked on an earlier decision to start reliever Bob Welch in Game 4. Instead, they would put Game 1 winner Burt Hooton back in to face Game 1 loser Bill Gullickson. Both Hooton and Gullickson would work on three days' rest, rather than the customary four.

Welch had pitched the entire regular season in 1981 as a starter, producing stellar results. Even though Welch was 9–5 with a 3.44 ERA, manager Tommy Lasorda decided to put him in the bullpen for the playoffs.

Picking Welch to pitch Game 4 would not have been a bad decision, but Lasorda went with experience in Hooton, who had been in the majors as a regular since 1972. Welch was in only his third season.

Expos manager Jim Fanning had been bandying about a similar idea: Scott Sanderson might pitch Game 4 because he had more rest than Gullickson. Sanderson had been solid during the regular season with a 9–5 record and a nifty 2.95 ERA. Yet, Fanning was skeptical after Sanderson lasted less than three innings and got rocked for four runs in his only 1981 playoff start — against the Phillies in the mini-series.

"It was argued that Scott Sanderson should have had the start in Game 4," teammate Ray Burris told me. "Bill was working on three days' rest in Game 4 and Sanderson wanted to pitch, with me following on the Sunday, if we lost in Game 4. Scott was available, but Scott didn't win the argument. As teammates, you push for someone like Scott because it was a team effort that got us to where we were. I didn't feel like I needed to say that to Jim, but I was acknowledging the energy Scott had put forth that season."

Lasorda's tinkering with the Dodgers' lineup didn't stop the decision to start Hooton. After being benched in the first three games of the series, veteran Rick Monday saw his name on the lineup card to play right field and, hopefully, add some offensive punch.

Ken Landreaux, Pedro Guerrero, and Dusty Baker had patrolled the Dodgers' outfield in the opening three contests, but Landreaux was the odd man out in Game 4 after going 1-for-10 over the three games. Lasorda wanted more zap and thought Monday would be the man. It was a decision that would take on special importance in the days to come. It turned out to be a prophetic move that would pay dividends for the Dodgers and wreak havoc for the Expos.

During the Dodgers' NLDS against the Houston Astros, Landreaux and Monday had been outfield regulars in each of the five games, along with Baker, because outfield mainstay Guerrero had to play third base while Ron Cey sat out the entire series with a finger injury.

Lasorda elected to go with the percentages in Landreaux for most of the Montreal series because Landreaux was 4-for-20 and Monday had been 3-for-14 against Houston. With Cey back in the Los Angeles lineup for the Expos series, however, Monday was the odd man out in the first three games as Guerrero switched back to his normal outfield position.

"I guess Tommy came to his senses," Monday said, joking years later about finally getting into the lineup. "In retrospect, I could have asked, 'How come you didn't do it earlier?' If I had said that, he would have said, 'Aw, shut up.' Here's the deal: everyone wants to play. It's frustrating. You would like to contribute more."

Something rather subtle and amusing took place late the night before Game 4 at the Sheraton Centre Hotel in Montreal and it was a bit of a rally booster for the Dodgers. After White's home run, a number of Los Angeles players retreated to a rooftop bar, and pitcher Jerry Reuss, who had coughed up the home run to White, decided to provide some comic relief. Reuss proceeded to take off his trousers and wear only his trench coat to slide down a railing, much to the delight of his mates.

"We were kind of drowning in our sorrows and trying to get over the loss," Monday said. "We were in a lounge near the top of the hotel. Jerry excuses himself to go to the washroom. He takes the spiral [stair] case up to the washroom. He yells out, 'Hey guys, think my coat is too short?' We laughed. In retrospect, we had lost a tough game and here was Jerry, who was taking the brunt of it, but he was trying to get us in a good mood."

In Game 4, as he had been in Game 1 in Los Angeles, Hooton was exemplary against the Expos; and Gullickson wasn't that shabby either.

In the third, with two out, Bill Russell reached on an error by third-baseman Larry Parrish and scored on a double to left by Dusty Baker to give the Dodgers a 1–0 lead.

In the fourth, the Expos tied the game in similar circumstances. Gary Carter reached on an error at third by Ron Cey. Jerry White walked and Warren Cromartie singled to score Carter. The Expos had the bases loaded when Hooton intentionally walked Chris Speier to pitch to Gullickson, but Gullickson was subsequently rung up by umpire Dutch Rennert.

This nail-biter continued 1–1 until the seventh, when the Dodgers broke loose to go ahead 3–1 on a two-run homer to left by Steve Garvey, after Baker had singled. The Dodgers put the game on ice in the ninth, scoring four runs with the help of Baker's two-run single and RBI base hits by Cey and the rarely used Reggie Smith.

Game 5 beckoned. The nail-biting would continue.

Chapter 19

Conspiracy Surrounds
Postponement of Game 5

T here was rain and more rain and some snowflakes thrown in on October 18 at Olympic Stadium, a day of mystery, suspense, subplots, and conspiracies.

This time two planes were waiting at Dorval Airport, but only one would go to New York. One was waiting to whisk the Expos away to New York; the other was waiting to whisk the Dodgers. But only the winners of Game 5 would make that trip: the losers would be going home.

It was a Sunday, and the series was all tied up at two games apiece. The final game would be sudden death.

The game was originally scheduled to start at 1:30 p.m., but NBC-TV requested that the game be switched to 4:00 p.m. to accommodate the network's National Football League coverage.

Sitting in the Dodgers' dugout before the game, Rick Monday chatted with rookie pitching sensation Fernando Valenzuela. Despite Valenzuela's limited English, Monday was able to coax some words out of the 19-year-old Mexican player, who would turn 20 the following month.

"Fernando was from a small village in Mexico, so I asked him if he had ever seen snow before," Monday said.

"In the mountains," Valenzuela said in broken English.

"He was blowing bubbles as we were working out," Monday said. "Here was a guy trying to catch snowflakes on his tongue. It was the age of innocence. It was really cold, but it didn't really bother him. Those are the things I remember from that day."

Monday tells the story of how he and the Dodgers, through sources, found out that Expos manager Jim Fanning was concerned about pitching Ray Burris on only three days' rest against Valenzuela and that Fanning was in no hurry to have the game played on the Sunday. Fanning, in essence, would have preferred to see Burris face Valenzuela on four days' rest on the Monday. Fanning also wanted to give his roughed-up bullpen a rest. If the game were delayed until Monday, though, it would also mean that Valenzuela would have four days' rest.

Fanning had cozied up to marketing employee Rodger Brulotte and requested that he not be in any hurry to start the game and requested, if possible, that the game be postponed, if necessary. Brulotte was responsible for a variety of roles, including setting up post-game interviews and calling the meteorologist for weather updates. Brulotte had initially been hired as a scouting assistant in 1970 but his titles and duties changed over the course of his employment.

"Fanning told Rodger Brulotte that he wasn't all that concerned about getting the game in that day — it was raining, cold," Monday recalled. "He told Brulotte not to use any excessive zeal in getting the game started as Brulotte called the airport weather service and was told the rain was about to let up in an hour.

"But then Brulotte went to the umpires, as a story was later reported, and he told them there was no chance, according to his information, that the rain would let up. So they gave him the benefit of the doubt and postponed it until the next day. Of course, after we sat there and waited all day, we went to the hotel, and it stopped raining."

At 7:30 a.m., due to the conflicting weather stories he was getting, National League president Chub Feeney called the game off and Expos public-address announcer Richard Morency told the fans that the game was being postponed.

Brulotte, much later in 2017, acknowledged to me that Monday's yarn was true.

"That is correct," Brulotte said. "I'll tell you what happened. It rained all day and I went up to Jim. He said if the game was postponed, it would mean Burris would have an extra day's rest. He said that if the game was postponed until the Monday that Burris and Steve Rogers would have more rest. Jim said that, 'If Ray is not going good, I have Rogers.'

"Jim and I would never have had the power to postpone the game. Chub Feeney made the decision. He called the weatherman himself for clarity and he was told it was going to rain for a while but that the rain would likely stop at 7:30. As it turned out, it stopped at 7:35."

Brulotte said he had figured rain wasn't all that bad for Montreal, and he remembered the witticism that *Boston Post* writer Gerald V. Hern had invented for Boston Braves pitching studs Warren Spahn and Johnny Sain: *Spahn, Sain, Then Pray for Rain.* But if Fanning was praying for rain, it was Brulotte who got Feeney to make the final call.

"Every time I saw Feeney afterward, he would say, 'How's the weatherman doing? How's the weatherman?'" Brulotte said, laughing.

And just so you know, Fanning and Brulotte kept the secret between them and the fence posts for years. It was remarkable that the bilingual Brulotte, who had many friends in the francophone media, didn't somehow spill the beans off the record to someone that day: somebody like, say, the venerable story-breaker Serge Touchette of *Le Journal de Montréal.*

Burris said 36 years later that he was unaware that this chatter was going on about Fanning wanting to get him more rest.

"Jim may have said that, but I didn't know that. I had no knowledge of that, but the powers-that-be were working on my behalf," Burris said. "Instead of pitching on three days' rest on the Sunday, I had four days' rest on Monday."

The postponement was a reprieve for Burris and Valenzuela, and also for legendary Dodgers announcer Vin Scully. The delay allowed Scully to get back to Montreal from Minneapolis, where he worked a National Football League game for NBC on the Sunday. Scully really hadn't wanted to leave the Dodgers, but a freelance contract with NBC meant he had to report to Minneapolis and do the play-by-play. Dodgers owner Peter O'Malley whisked Scully back and forth between Montreal and Minneapolis on his private plane.

"Vin wanted to be there in Montreal and we wanted him to be there," O'Malley said.

On the field before the game in Minneapolis, Vikings general manager Jim Murray was teasing Scully, wondering if he would rather be in Montreal calling play-by-play of the Dodgers game.

"You must be really torn," Murray said to Scully.

"I don't even want to think about the Dodgers game," Scully had replied. "I've got a football game to do and I will not be distracted." And then, for some reason, he says, he added, "And you know what? It might rain."

Murray then replied, "If it's rained out, just so you can go back there and do the game, I'll believe there's a Dodger in the Sky."

Up high in the press box in his booth, the technical staff was teasing Scully, too. But he bluffed them off. "Fellas, I'd love to know what is going on there, but I don't want anyone to feed me a score. I'm trying to block it all out."

During the game, someone passed on the word to Scully that the Dodgers-Expos game was postponed because of rain. "I said, 'Wow! The Big Dodger in the Sky.' So I flew back to Montreal. I didn't see Murray again, but I guarantee that it had to shake him up to see that Game 5 was rained out. That was one in a million."

For the Expos, the postponement was hardly good news. It sure would have been a good time to have a roof on the Big O so the game wouldn't have been delayed, with 50,000 fans milling about the stadium.

"When it was postponed, I didn't have a good feeling when I left the ballpark," Warren Cromartie told me in 2017. "It meant extra rest for Valenzuela."

The Expos spent most of the day looking at the puddles of rain, and, to break the monotony, veteran Larry Parrish asked rookie Terry Francona to dive into a pool of water for the photographers and cameramen. When one cameraman asked for more of the same, Francona dove a second time.

"I don't remember the rain so much, but I remember the delay, delay, delay," Expos owner Charles Bronfman said.

Chapter 20

Game 5: The Big One

T he next day, the Monday, Rick Monday showed up and looked at the early crowd coming into the stadium. Later, as he came out for the Dodgers' warm-ups and then for the start of the game, he didn't see many people. He was elated. Compared to 54,372 for Game 3 of the series and 54,499 for Game 4, this crowd for Game 5 was not anywhere near the 50,000 range. The final head count was 36,491.

Many people were wondering, *Where is everybody?* Yes, it was the beginning of the week, so people had to work, but couldn't people play hooky and come and watch one of the most anticipated games in Canadian baseball history? Baseball was supposed to be a national obsession in Canada, but especially in Quebec and Montreal, so a crowd of 36,000 and change was certainly puzzling and didn't cut it.

Monday was pleasantly surprised.

> Sounds can be deafening. Over 50,000 people don't care for us but you don't take it personal. When you're playing in the outfield, not the infield, with the noise from the crowd, you can't hear what the other guys are saying.

That's why for the final game, just over 35,000 showed up so it's not as deafening as the noise of the previous games.

The cavernous stadium was far from full. With 20,000 fewer people in attendance than for either of the previous two games, I had to wonder whether baseball was that important to the people of Montreal. I don't mean to sound harsh, but a trip to the World Series was on the line. It gave our team a bit of a mental boost, as if some of the hostility of the home crowd had been sucked out of the stadium.

Yes, much less "*Val-deri, val-dera*." Much less of "The Happy Wanderer."

"The stands seemed empty. The stands were not jammed," Monday said. "It was horrible. I understand why. People had to work and fans came in from outside just for the weekend and when the game was postponed on the Sunday, they left the city."

That same day in the *Montreal Gazette*, the Canadian Imperial Bank of Commerce was promoting Registered Retirement Savings Plan term deposits at a glowing rate of 17 percent. The interest rate for borrowing money, though, was at a staggering 22 percent. Remember that?

It was also a day when the ritzy Ritz Carlton Hotel in Montreal was playing host to a number of premiers from provinces from across Canada intent on getting a full conference for new talks on the Canadian constitution and the British North America Act.

So with the regularly scheduled time of 1:30 still on, Ray Burris strode to the mound for the Expos to face the top of the Dodgers' order in Davey Lopes. Burris was coming off a tremendous effort in Game 2 in Los Angeles, when he had blanked the Dodgers on five hits in a 3–0 win.

Lopes promptly popped up to catcher Gary Carter, bringing up Bill Russell, whose signature batting style was fashionably choking way up on the bat about an inch and a half. He fell behind 0–2 but fought back patiently to work the count to full. Then he slapped the sixth pitch past first-baseman Warren Cromartie just inside the bag into the right-field corner for a triple. Burris overcame this problem by getting Dusty Baker to ground out to third and getting Steve Garvey on a slow comebacker to the mound.

In the bottom half of the inning, leadoff hitter Tim Raines doubled to left centre and would have had a triple had Baker not taken the ball off the fence on one bounce. More than one bounce and Raines would have gone to third. Lucky bounce for the Dodgers. Raines had already rounded second when he jammed on the brakes, realizing he wouldn't make it safely.

Rodney Scott came to the plate and laid a sacrifice bunt down the third-base line. Valenzuela pounced on the ball and threw to Cey at third to try to nab Raines, but Raines slid in ahead of the throw. Third-base umpire Eric Gregg got down on one knee and flashed the safe sign far and wide for everyone to see. Russell didn't like the call and neither did manager Tommy Lasorda, who came storming out to let Gregg know his views. The play was officially ruled a fielder's choice. Funny thing is, the play saw Bobby Castillo start warming up in the Dodgers' bullpen. And it was only the first inning. Crazy.

With men on first and third, Scott pulled off a doozy of a play. After Valenzuela threw his first pitch to Andre Dawson, the third batter, Scott started running to second but pulled up short, teasing the Dodgers and hoping they would throw to second and allow Raines to go home. Daredevil Scott purposely got in a rundown and then somehow dove back to first head-first, safe. But Raines didn't go.

What didn't happen next is that Scott didn't try to really steal second, to put two runners in scoring position for Dawson and avoid a potential double play. Scott had the jets to take off and steal bases with ease, but he stayed at first. Odd. Dawson got jammed with a pitch and hit a lazy high hopper to second. Lopes threw to Russell for one out and the throw back to first to Garvey completed the double play. Raines scored and the Expos were up 1–0.

The game stayed that way until the fifth inning when the Dodgers finally got to Burris. Monday singled to centre and scampered to third when Pedro Guerrero singled to right. This was trouble for the Expos. Burris got a breather when Mike Scioscia lined out to Scott at second. The runners stayed put. One man was out and there were still men on first and third.

With Valenzuela at the plate, the Expos' infield played back at double-play depth with one out. Burris threw a wild pitch but he got lucky when Carter was able to keep the ball from bouncing no more than a few feet down the third-base line. Monday stayed at third but Guerrero scooted to second.

Somehow, the Expos' infield strategy should have changed, but it didn't. With the possibility of a double play erased, the infield wasn't playing in for a play at the plate, preferring to stay back at normal depth. Crazy. Bad strategy. The Expos were prepared to play their infield back and let a run score? Ever heard of the old baseball expression "Give up a run"? Somebody screwed up here. Fanning, maybe?

Traditionally in the early-to-mid innings, teams tend to give up a run rather than try to nail a runner at the plate, but this game was sudden death. In the middle of a game with all the marbles on the table and the Expos up 1–0, with planes waiting at the airport for New York, and runs hard to come by all series, the Expos' infield should have played in, don't you think?

First base was open, but there was no way the Expos were going to issue an intentional walk to Valenzuela to load the bases and present another double-play opportunity with Lopes, the leadoff hitter, on deck.

Third-baseman Larry Parrish said that scenario took place "too long ago" and that he had no recollection of it.

Valenzuela, a surprisingly solid hitter for a pitcher, chopped a ball in between second and first. Scott, playing way out on the outfield Astroturf, with no chance to get Monday at the plate, underhanded the ball to Cromartie at first for the out. Monday scored to tie the game 1–1, but Guerrero stayed at second.

Again, what were the Expos doing? They were playing at normal depth when they should have been playing in at the edge of the infield grass on the dirt or at least parallel to the bases on the dirt so they could cut off Monday at the plate, if necessary. Little or nothing was said in the media at the time about this blunder.

"I remember going first to third and Fernando knocked in the run with a 45-footer," Monday recalled, clearly.

Valenzuela had made excellent contact during the regular season as a hitter. He was no easy out. While most pitchers normally hit anywhere between .100 and .150, Valenzuela batted a surprising .250 with 16 hits in 64 at-bats. Even still, the Expos should have had the infield in to try to keep the Dodgers from scoring with men on second and third. You didn't need to be a Philadelphia lawyer to figure that out. Not doing so was probably a huge mistake.

Of course, it's all hypothetical, but if the Expos had played in, Scott would have had ample time to take Valenzuela's grounder, check Monday at third, and then throw to Cromartie for out number two.

If you thought that was confounding, just think that Guerrero stayed at second even though Valenzuela's bouncer was way over between second and first.

Then, with two out and Baker ready at second, Speier booted a ball at short and Lopes reached on the error. This time, Guerrero moved to third. But Burris got out of the inning with no further damage by getting Bill Russell to ground out to Speier.

This nail-biter continued, the tie score still unchanged in the Expos' seventh. At that point, after Dawson popped up to second and Carter struck out, Parrish doubled, bringing Game 3 home run hero Jerry White to the plate with a man on. Dodgers manager Tommy Lasorda was taking no chances. Against southpaw Jerry Reuss in Game 3, the righty-swinging White had hit a go-ahead three-run homer. So in an eerily similar situation, Lasorda had Valenzuela issue White an intentional base on balls. The strategy worked. Valenzuela induced Cromartie to pop up to the catcher for the third out.

The suspense continued in the Expos' eighth inning when Fanning made a momentous decision. He sent in Tim Wallach to pinch-hit for Burris, who was sailing along in his second consecutive masterpiece against Valenzuela in the series and was not apparently tired. While Speier was at the plate to lead off the inning, Burris knelt in the on-deck circle wearing a huge blue winter jacket, expecting to bat for himself.

When Speier was retired by Valenzuela on a fly to centre, Fanning motioned to umpire Harry Wendelstedt that Wallach was coming in. Burris walked dejectedly to the dugout. Wallach grounded out back to Valenzuela.

"Taking out Burris was a bad decision, because he was pitching good the whole game. Burris didn't want to come out," Rowland Office recalled.

"It was a tough moment. I felt like I was getting stronger and I think the Dodgers were aware of it," Burris said. "I was in a groove. I was in a rhythm. I had a purpose in mind and that was to win the game. No, I didn't want to come out [of] the game. You plead the case, but at the end of the case, the manager ends the conversation."

Working on four days' rest because of Sunday's postponement, Burris looked sharp even though Fanning told reporters later that he thought the pitcher was tiring. But Burris's performance had made the postponement look good even if there was a conspiracy between Fanning, Rodger Brulotte, and the weatherman. Likewise, Valenzuela was fantastic on four days' rest.

"Look at the game Burris gave us. He gave us a heckuva game," Brulotte said.

And who should be summoned from the bullpen to replace Burris? Keep reading. The stage was set for heavy-duty drama in the top of the ninth. And Monday would have a huge part in it. So would Steve Rogers.

Chapter 21

Monday, Blue Monday, and That Hit

Rick Monday had become an elder statesman, a journeyman, an ancient mariner, by the time spring training began in 1981 in Vero Beach, Florida. There had been speculation that Monday, because he was no longer being used as a full-time player, might call it quits following the 1981 season. Even he was starting to get the message.

Teammates and officials suggested that the affable, eloquent grey eminence might be better suited for a position as an announcer on radio or television. Monday even approached Dodgers general manager Al Campanis to tell him that the 1981 season could possibly be his last. Campanis, acting on a hunch, told Monday to wait.

"With that tremendous voice, we knew he was going to be an announcer," recalled Dodgers pitching coach Ron Perranoski in 2016.

All through the 1981 regular season and for much of the playoffs, Monday was a highly- paid spectator on the bench — $280,000 per annum — as evidenced by the 130 at-bats he accumulated during 66 games of the strike-fragmented regular season. At 35, he had grown accustomed to handing out advice to younger players about the intricacies and nuances of the game.

Monday was used to part-time duty and to holding down a spot on the bench, and he had begun to develop a quasi-stooped posture. Nevertheless, on occasion he could still rise up and make significant contributions.

In the deciding game of the National League Division Series against the Houston Astros, Monday had faced feared fireballer Nolan Ryan. On an 0–2 count, tough against any pitcher, let alone Ryan, Monday managed to get his bat around quickly enough to slap a single into right, scoring what would become the winning run in a 4–0 Los Angeles victory propelled by Jerry Reuss's complete-game five-hitter.

"When you see Ryan out there, you might be better going to the dugout and checking out the menu for the restaurant after the game," Monday told me, chuckling.

So what happened to Monday in the first three games of the NLCS against the Expos, given his splendid contribution against the Astros? He was benched. He made one appearance, a pinch-hit effort that led to an out in Game 2. He did not appear at all in either Game 1 or Game 3.

So much for having been a hero in the Houston series: Monday's reward was one at-bat in the first three games against the Expos. But the tide was about to turn.

After the Expos established the 2–1 series lead in Game 3, Dodgers manager Tommy Lasorda had told reporters he expected to put Monday into the lineup for Game 4. He did, and Monday went 1-for-4, prompting Lasorda to leave his veteran in the lineup for the deciding Game 5. Once again, fate called upon Monday to become the man in the clutch, much as he had been in the deciding game against Houston.

His moment came in the top of the ninth inning of Game 5. It sent the Dodgers to the World Series and broke the hearts of baseball fans all across Canada.

Monday isn't one for bragging, so he admits he has seldom seen the video of his home run off of Steve Rogers — five times at most, he says — and only when others have shown it to him.

The YouTube clip starts with Monday walking out from the Dodgers' third-base side at Olympic Stadium toward home plate on his right. Standing at home plate is umpire Harry Wendelstedt and crouched down is Expos catcher Gary Carter.

As Monday walks toward the batter's box, Wendelstedt says something to him. The Dodgers outfielder, oblivious to his surroundings, just keeps walking, into the batter's box. In the Expos' dugout, manager Jim Fanning is seen standing up, looking worried as coach Ozzie Virgil Sr. sits beside him.

Finding himself in the unfamiliar role of relief pitcher, Rogers had come on in the top of the ninth and erased the first two batters he faced. Steve Garvey was retired on an easy popup to second, bringing Ron Cey to the plate. Cey worked Rogers to a 3–0 count, prompting NBC play-by-play man Dick Enberg to say, "[Expos shortstop] Chris Speier, with a whistle, got the attention of the infield, and Rogers, and said, hey, he may be swinging. Be alert."

Cey didn't swing away on the 3–0 count. He took a strike down the middle of the plate. With the count 3–1, Cey hit a dangerous-looking fly ball to the warning track in left but Tim Raines hauled it in. Cey had started to do one of those backup trots toward first base, just like Carlton Fisk did in the 1975 World Series, but then he realized Raines had caught it. Cey headed back to the dugout. On the mound Rogers shook his head, realizing Cey had almost hit the ball out.

"Ron Cey, when it left that bat … and that, too, might have been a home run in Dodger Stadium," Enberg told his listeners after Raines caught the ball. "It might have been a home run on a warmer day, too," commented Enberg's colour analyst Tom Seaver. "A good swing. It looks like he was right on it. Dick, you can see Ron Cey with almost the same kind of actions that Carlton Fisk had in that great World Series between Cincinnati and Boston. But warning track power. Raines had it easily, right on the warning track."

Enberg chimed in: "Just a couple metres shy."

Then, in the video, up steps Monday. He takes long looks at Rogers, who preferred to peer down at the ground rather than look toward home plate. In a scary moment for Rogers and the Expos, Monday gets wood on Rogers's first offering and snaps it sharply back into the stands behind home plate, but Monday was just a little under the pitch.

"Rick's had some excellent swings these last two games," Enberg comments.

Rogers clearly doesn't want to give Monday anything good to hit. He purposely appears to throw three consecutive lob balls while Expos fans

A fly ball to Andre Dawson. And deep. Dawson to the track, Dawson to the wall. It's gone, a home run by Rick Monday. Look at the scene at home plate. Holy moly. And the Dodgers go wild. The veteran outfielder clears the centre-field fence and the Dodgers lead 2–1.
— Dodgers play-by-play voice Vin Scully describing Rick Monday's home run, October 19, 1981 (Permission: MLB Productions)

plead with him to nail down the final out. The urgency in their voices rises with every pitch, until the count is 3–1.

And that is the moment when Monday got something he could hit. He knocks the ball into right-centre field, a lazy fly ball that Andre Dawson seems poised to catch. Monday looks way up in an attempt to see the ball he's just hit. So does Rogers and everyone else in the park. But as Dawson drifts back toward the fence, the ball just keeps floating, floating, until there is nothing Dawson can do but watch it carry over the fence.

The video of that historic moment shows Dawson moving back toward the high fence at the Big O, then realizing he has no chance of catching the ball. He is about to attempt a jump and then stops.

"The roof was open, the sun was shining, and Monday was hitting in the shadows," recalled Dodgers pitcher Jerry Reuss. "The ball went high into the area highlighted by the sun. I watched as Dawson went from the turf to the track to the wall."

In their half of the final inning, two men out, the Expos did get two men on, but suddenly it was all over. The Dodgers were headed to the World Series. The Expos were going home.

That single moment still burns in the hearts of Expos fans and players everywhere. Many were crying, holding their heads in their hands and woollen mitts, disbelieving.

This was supposed to be the Expos' year, their best-ever crack at the World Series. Instead, it will always be remembered as the year of Blue Monday, when the dreams were shattered on a cold Monday afternoon, by a home run struck by an amazed Rick Monday.

As he ran past first base toward second, the left-handed Monday thrust his left arm into the air much like a prizefighter, and when he rounded second base, he repeated the gesture, this time with inconsolable Expos shortstop Chris Speier looking down in shock, bent over with hands on knees.

As he rounded third, Monday didn't use his left arm but raised his right arm to slap the right hand of third-base coach Danny Ozark and both immediately clasped hands, prompting Ozark to perform a pirouette to his left. By now, the Dodgers' dugout had emptied as players poured out to congratulate Monday at home plate. Monday recalls,

> I knew I had hit it good but I thought it was going to be an out. Then I thought it might hit high off the fence for a triple. It's a very high wall. I looked at Andre, and then at the last second I looked back at the ball, just seconds before it disappeared.
>
> It was a bit above belt-high on the inside of the plate. You try to look for a pitch you can drive in a situation like that with men in scoring position. You try to move them over; but with the bases empty, you try to drive it — on the first two pitches anyway. In a big game like that, you don't expect to get a pitch you can drive. I fouled off a good pitch from Rogers and I didn't expect to see another. I was a little surprised to see a ball I could drive.
>
> I had been expecting a sinkerball, but Rogers, not wanting to walk me, happened to elevate the fastball. But I still had to hit it. I hit it really hard. It's tough to hit a ball out of that stadium. I didn't think it was a home run day. When I looked at the trajectory of Ron Cey's fly ball, I thought it had a chance of going out. Raines was backing up and then he came in. I made a mental comment, *Geez, that ball is going nowhere.* Cey hit it extremely good and the weather wasn't warm.
>
> When I hit the ball, I didn't know where in hell it went. I couldn't find the seam of the ball. I saw the outfielders going for it. Near the wall, I saw a sudden flash of the ball. When Andre didn't look over the wall, I knew it was out of the park. I was stunned. I almost fell down between

second and third. Without a doubt, it was the biggest hit of my big-league career. No hit had more impact than that one because of the immediacy of the stage that was set — the Yankees were waiting in New York.

Years later, Monday looked down at the briefcase lying in front of him with clips of information for his upcoming Dodgers broadcasts. But there was something else in there — statistics indicating the number of pitchers he had faced during a solid career in the big leagues.

"I have a printout here of all the pitchers I faced in my 19 seasons," Monday told me. "There were 502 pitchers and I can tell you without looking at the number that I'd be surprised if I hit over .200 against Rogers. In all, there were 74 at-bats and I only managed to hit two home runs against him."

Close to 40 years after his epic home run against Rogers, Monday still kept those statistics in his briefcase. Imagine.

Back in the sombre quietness of the Expos' clubhouse, Rogers was trying to explain it all. "There are only two pitches that Rick Monday can hit out of the park: a hanging slider or hanging sinker," Rogers said. "I wanted to throw him a sinker low and away. I wanted to pitch around him. I was off base. The sinker hung. Perhaps I'm being hard on myself, but it's not going to have a lasting effect. It seems like Death Valley right now but it's not. This one game will be a little harder to forget than the performances of the past month. If that's not human nature, I've missed the beat somewhere."

Then a desolate Rogers looked to Shakespeare and the dramatic arts. "Are you aware of the two masks that signify comedy and tragedy?" Rogers asked reporters quietly. "Monday got the smile. And I got stuck with the frown."

Rogers has reflected often about that home run. He has always been courteous in fielding questions, never shying away. He faces the music head-on whenever reporters and fans talk to him about it. But no matter how you cut it, he was out of his element this time.

"As a starter, you're trying to work into the flow of the game," Rogers said in 2017. "As a reliever, when you don't channel your energy, your adrenalin goes crazy and your mechanics jump out of rhythm. That little twist of not being able to channel this extra energy can undo you.

"Did I handle the extra adrenalin? I did not. It made me quicker, and that quickness was defeating my sinker. I wasn't on top of it. What should have been my best pitch, wasn't. The adrenalin was pumping so hard."

The willies, the nerves, and the butterflies were having an emotional, negative effect on Rogers. He was carrying the weight of a city, a province, and a nation on his shoulders; so, probing a little further, I asked, "You mean your heart was beating too fast?"

"Yeah, that's what I mean," he said. "I couldn't back off. My heart was just pounding. Earlier in the inning, I had thrown pitches that were not very good. Cey's fly ball was the exact same pitch, a bad sinker. He just got under it, a bit."

The sinkerball was Rogers's bread-and-butter pitch, one where he says he uses his index finger and snaps his wrist to the right. "Nobody really taught me that," he said. "It was God-given ability. I learned that pitch when I was nine years old. With Monday, I threw a 3–1 pitch down the middle and he did what he had to do and hit the ball out. Gary Carter and I were completely on the same page. I thought down and away. If I throw too low and away, I walk him. Guerrero was up next and he wasn't hitting the ball."

Indeed, he wasn't. In fact, Guerrero was 5-for-36 in the 1981 post-season at that point, including a 2-for-19 skid against the Expos. He was really in a deep funk, but there was no way Rogers was going to throw an intentional ball on a 3–1 pitch to Monday in order to pitch to Guerrero, even if Guerrero was scuffling at the plate.

"If you intentionally walk him, there's blood in the water and the sharks come in," Rogers said. "I made a poor pitch. And I didn't execute. When Monday hit it, I thought that with the damp and cold it was way out but maybe not all the way out. When I looked again, I lost all hope."

Dawson chasing back. Still on the run. At the fence. Trouble. Home run Monday. 2–1 Dodgers. Rick Monday with a solo home run in the top of the ninth inning and a 2–1 lead for the Dodgers.
— Expos play-by-play voice Dave Van Horne describing Rick Monday's home run, October 19, 1981 (Permission: MLB Productions)

"I'm not close enough to a major media centre to say I've been asked about the home run thousands of times, but it would be hundreds of times. The pitch was not my career. It was an important part of my career, but it was not the defining point of my career. But what I did will forever be in the record books."

The home run was similar to the one Bobby Thomson of the New York Giants hit off of Brooklyn Dodgers pitcher Ralph Branca almost exactly 30 years earlier, in 1951, at the Polo Grounds in New York. Branca was so distraught after the game that he got down on the clubhouse steps and said, "Why me? Why me?"

As it turns out, Rogers struck out Guerrero to end the inning. Go figure.

As others weighed in, there were some interesting opinions about the ball as it was hit into one of the deepest parts of the Big O's vast terrain.

"It was a routine fly ball to centre. It just carried. It kept on going," said long-time Expos scouting assistant and broadcaster Rodger Brulotte. "It wasn't a Willie Stargell home run, an Andre Dawson home run, or a Vladimir Guerrero home run. It barely made it over the fence. It reminds me of the home run Rick Dempsey of the Dodgers hit against Dennis Martinez of the Expos in the 22-inning game in 1989. Martinez came on in relief like Rogers. It was the same as the Rogers-Monday situation except that the Dempsey home run was during the regular season."

In the words of Expos hurler Ray Burris, "Rogers was a good sinkerball pitcher, who happened to leave that pitch up to Monday. It looked like a regular fly ball to Dawson when he hit it off the bat."

Expos third-baseman Larry Parrish noted that "Olympic Stadium had a sort of egg-shaped roof and when the wind came over the stadium in centre field, it seemed to swish the ball down. You didn't see many home runs go out of Olympic Stadium in centre field. And that day, you had to really crush it to get it out of the ballpark. So with Dawson patrolling centre field, he seemed to run everything down. When Monday hit that ball, you knew it was hit good, but you didn't think it was going out. You knew that Hawk would get to it. I'm looking out there, and I figure it's just going to be a long out. And then it just disappeared over the wall. I said, 'What?' What a shock."

How and why Rogers came in to pitch in relief is one of those base-ball puzzlers that will be discussed forever. Rogers was a career starter,

SEQUENCE OF PITCHES TO MONDAY FROM ROGERS

First pitch: foul ball into seats behind home plate
Second pitch: ball outside
Third pitch: ball outside
Fourth pitch: ball at the shoelaces
Fifth pitch: home run to right-centre

unaccustomed to coming in late in a game to pitch only an inning or two. On Friday, October 16, he had already hurled a masterful Game 3 of the series as the Expos beat the Dodgers 4–1 on Jerry White's three-run homer.

Speaking recently with me about that game, Monday suggested, "I don't think the mayor of Montreal will plan a celebration for me anytime soon."

Asked if he was surprised that manager Jim Fanning hadn't brought in a lefty like Bill Lee or Woodie Fryman to face him, Monday deflected the question. "Steve Rogers started the inning," he replied. "Ray Burris had thrown eight strong innings. He was a great guy I had played with when I was with the Cubs. He had pitched a heckuva game, but there was nothing wrong with the pitching change. It was a surprise to see Steve warm up, but he was a really good pitcher. He could control a game. You had to alter your approach with him. When I saw him warming up, I said, 'Oh, geez, what if he takes over?'"

"All the conditions for trouble were there," Rogers said recently. "I just had pitched the third game, as tough a game as any pitcher has thrown with a championship on the line. I very much wanted to lock into pitching in Game 5. I honestly thought about it and analyzed the situation, especially as the rainout now allowed Valenzuela to come back on four days' rest."

So while the rain and snow and sleet were pounding down on Sunday, Rogers approached Fanning and pitching coach Galen Cisco to tell them he was available to pitch in Game 5, if ever it came to that, on only two days' rest, in relief.

"We had already talked about it, that Monday was my throw day on the side," Rogers said. "My arm was not sore. And physically, I was 100 percent ready."

BLUE MONDAY, OCTOBER 19, 1981
LOS ANGELES DODGERS

Players	AB	R	H	RBI	BB	SO	PO	A
Lopes 2b	4	0	1	0	0	0	3	3
Russell ss	4	0	2	0	0	0	2	3
Baker rf	4	0	0	0	0	0	0	0
Garvey 1b	4	0	0	0	0	0	10	0
Cey 3b	3	0	0	0	1	0	0	2
Monday rf	4	2	2	1	0	1	0	0
Landreaux rf	0	0	0	0	0	0	1	0
Guerrero cf	4	0	1	0	0	1	4	0
Scioscia c	3	0	0	0	0	0	7	0
Valenzuela p	3	0	0	1	0	0	0	1
Welch p	0	0	0	0	0	0	0	0
Totals	33	2	6	2	1	2	27	9

Fielding
DP: 1. Lopes-Russell-Garvey
Batting
3B: Russell (1, off Burris)
HR: Monday (1, 9th inning off Rogers, 0 on, 2 out)
GDP: Guerrero (4, off Burris)
Team LOB: 5
SB: Lopes (5, 2nd base off Burris/Carter)

MONTREAL EXPOS

Players	AB	R	H	RBI	BB	SO	PO	A
Raines lf	4	1	1	0	0	1	2	0
Scott 2b	3	0	0	0	0	0	3	5
Dawson cf	4	0	0	0	0	1	4	0
Carter c	3	0	1	0	1	1	3	1
Manuel pr	0	0	0	0	0	0	0	0
Parrish 3b	3	0	1	0	1	0	1	1

White rf	3	0	0	0	1	1	2	0
Cromartie 1b	3	0	0	0	0	0	0	5
Speier ss	3	0	0	0	0	0	0	5
Burris p	2	0	0	0	0	1	0	1
Wallach ph	1	0	0	0	0	0	0	0
Rogers p	0	0	0	0	0	0	0	0
Totals	29	1	3	0	3	5	15	18

Fielding
DP: 1. Speier-Scott-Cromartie
E: Speier (2)
Batting
2B: Raines (2, off Valenzuela); Parrish (2, off Valenzuela)
SH: Scott (1, off Valenzuela)
GDP: Dawson (2, off Valenzuela)
IBB: White (1, by Valenzuela)
Team LOB: 5

Pitching

Los Angeles	IP	H	R	ER	BB	SO	HR	BFP
Valenzuela W (1–1)	8.2	3	1	1	3	6	0	32
Welch SV (1)	0.1	0	0	0	0	0	0	1
Totals	9	3	1	1	3	6	0	33

IBB: Valenzuela (1, White)
Inherited runners: scored: Welch 2–0

Montreal Expos	IP	H	R	ER	BB	SO	HR	BFP
Burris	8	5	1	1	1	1	0	30
Rogers L (1–1)	1	1	1	1	0	1	1	4
Totals	9	6	2	2	1	2	1	34

WP: Burris (1)
Umpires: HP – Harry Wendelstedt, 1B – Joe West, 2B – Paul Pryor
3B – Eric Gregg, LF – Paul Runge, RF – Dutch Rennert
Time of game: 2:41
Attendance: 36,491

Source: retrosheet.org

Rick Monday looks up at the ball he hit as it heads for the fence.

Steve Rogers looks up to see the ball hit by Rick Monday.

Yet, there were other pitchers also ready to go into the game: lefties Fryman and Lee and right-handers such as Scott Sanderson, Elias Sosa, and, of course, Jeff Reardon, who had been warming up beside Rogers in the bullpen. Right-hander Stan Bahnsen was unavailable because of a hamstring injury.

"Had we played on the Sunday, I still wonder what would have happened," Parrish said. "At that particular time, Valenzuela had come from nowhere to become some kind of wonder kid, the rookie of the year. He had that devastating screwball. However, he wasn't rested enough to pitch on Sunday, but now, because we were rained out or snowed out, he was able to come out on Monday and pitch on four days' rest. So many ifs, so many second guesses. Reardon, at the time, was our closer, but I think he was experiencing back problems. He really wasn't able to pitch that day. Jim thought Steve was our best pitcher, given the circumstances."

At that point in the conversation, Parrish chuckled and said, "With starting pitchers, the old vernacular holds that you've got to get them early before they can settle in. Relievers are used to being out there for an inning, a shorter period of time, whereas the starter's mentality is conditioned to go at least six or seven innings.

"The good thing about baseball is that you have 162 games and probably 100 of them are what-ifs, whether you are a fan or the media. What if he had done this or done that? You could be lying in bed in the middle of the night thinking about it. Anybody who likes jigsaw puzzles is going to love the game of baseball. It's like studying the horseracing form, puzzling over the winners and losers. And complaining when you get it wrong."

Over in the Dodgers' clubhouse, veteran Dusty Baker motioned for rookies Steve Sax and Tom Niedenfuer to join him for a few words of wisdom. He put his arms around both players. "C'mere, rooks," he bellowed, as only Baker could. "You guys are the luckiest guys in the whole world. Did you know that Ernie Banks and Dick Allen never played in a World Series? But you guys will be going to your first World Series in your first year. You are very lucky. But Mo?" he said, referring to Monday. "He deserves every World Series he gets into. Mo has paid his dues. I mean, he deserves them."

Watching on the television at home like many others were Donald Fehr, general counsel to the players association, and executive director Marvin Miller.

"Steve was fairly involved in the negotiations to end the strike," Fehr said. "Steve was called in to pitch. I remember it like it was yesterday. It was somebody you know. I could feel it in my stomach. It was an opportunity for Steve to be a hero and throw good. Starting pitchers don't usually come in for short relief. I mean, in any sport, when you come down to the end, you have extraordinary players battling it out. Somebody has to win, somebody has to lose."

Monday won, Rogers lost. Like the ancient mariner, Monday started his journey with solid success, then got bogged down as he rode the pine. But not on this day. He stepped up and became a hero. It was the game of his lifetime. It just doesn't get much better than that.

Chapter 22

Cromartie Reduced to Tears

T he Dodgers were celebrating on the field at Olympic Stadium. Still sitting in disbelief on the long bench of the Expos' dugout were Chris Speier and Florida amigos Warren Cromartie, Andre Dawson, and Tim Raines. For close to an hour, they stared out at an empty field.

"We were soaking up things," Cromartie recalled.

Soaking up the reality of not going to the World Series.

Finally, they all decided to go to the clubhouse, where the doom and despair would continue. The normally exuberant, animated Cromartie was reduced to tears. Cromartie was always the Expos' loud resident chatterbox in the clubhouse, but not this time. The scene was caught in still photographs, following policy that allows photographers to enter clubhouses after the end of a playoff series but not following a regular-season game.

"I've never seen a group of athletes so crushed. Cromartie was speechless," *Montreal Gazette* sports columnist Tim Burke wrote the next day.

"We were completely numb, completely numb," Cromartie said close to 40 years later. "We had it in our grasp. We put our hearts out. It was absolutely one of the worst moments you could have."

Warren Cromartie in the clubhouse after the Blue Monday loss.

And when I asked Cromartie if he had ever been in such an emotional state before, he replied, "I'd never felt like that since that day in Little League. I hadn't felt like that in a long time."

Cromartie was referring to an event years earlier, in about 1965, in his hometown of Miami. It was a Little League game when he would have been around 12 years old.

"I had hit a home run and I forgot to touch third base," Cromartie said glumly. "The other team got the ball back and made the appeal throw to third and I was called out."

Cromartie had been heartbroken then, just as he was that cold fall afternoon in Montreal.

The photo of an emotional Cromartie in this chapter, taken by John Mahoney of the *Montreal Gazette*, is rarely seen now. It did appear on the front page of the paper the day after the loss. Canadian Press photographer Bill Grimshaw came up with a similar photo that was distributed by his news agency, but it, too, got little or no play. Intruding on someone in a private hellish moment was tough to do, but Grimshaw felt a need to do it.

"I still remember the shot," Grimshaw said. "A lot of papers never used it. I sort of felt bad but I wasn't backing off. I went hard on him. I probably took 20 pictures, not a full roll. It was a helluva good picture. I still feel sorry for him, but they were paying me money to get pictures like that. I was close to full frame. There is no remorse on my part. It was a good picture. I wasn't going to miss it. I know most people wouldn't have the guts, but I know a good losing dressing room."

"A good losing dressing room" was a good way to sum up the clubhouse.

"It took a while to get over it in Montreal," Cromartie said. "I didn't sleep that night. The next day, I just wanted to get out of Montreal as fast as I could.

"When I saw Rick Monday hit that ball, I knew it was hit pretty good. When he went past me at first base celebrating, it was not a good feeling. I was hoping Hawk would get out there and catch the ball. We called him Hawk because he would run down most balls."

Cromartie said Dodgers manager Tommy Lasorda merely took advantage of an inexperienced manager in Jim Fanning when Fanning probably should have brought in Woodie Fryman or Bill Lee in a lefty-versus-lefty situation against Monday.

"Steve Rogers had been the senior guy. He was a big stopper, but he was not a reliever. Jim went with his guts, his gut feeling," Cromartie said. "Dick Williams was a manager. He knew how to do flip-flops. Dick would have made a difference. Fryman and Lee were available. Jim could have made the switch. Monday had just missed a home run on a foul ball."

In hindsight, wouldn't most managers have lifted Rogers and replaced him with Lee or Fryman after Monday hit the foul ball, or after Ron Cey went to the warning track? Cey seemed so confident when he hit the ball that was caught by Raines that he backed up, way up and off in foul territory, before realizing Raines was going to get to it.

If Dick Williams had been the manager, he very likely would never have used Rogers in relief, period.

If it was any consolation, to heal the wounds and the emotions, Davey Lopes and Ron Cey of the Dodgers came into the Expos' clubhouse to shake the hands of the Expos' players.

"I'll never forget that," Cromartie said about the two Dodgers showing up.

"Gary Carter and I went to the Dodgers' clubhouse and shook hands with them," Expos shortstop Chris Speier related when I told him the yarn about Lopes and Cey.

All over the clubhouse there were dumbfounded Expos. Their hearts broken, their eyes misty, their thoughts of depression sifting in all directions. They saw their hopes of going to New York to start the World Series dashed. The Expos' chartered plane never took off for the Big Apple.

"That was the biggest disappointment of my career," Expos third-baseman Larry Parrish was saying, years later.

Dick Enberg: Steve Rogers has fallen behind here, two balls and one strike. Three and one. Saw Monday point at the ball after it landed in the dirt and it's thrown out of play. Three and one, the outfield is deep toward right. Rodney Scott, the second-baseman, way out beyond the line, as you can see, trying to cut off the hole between first and second.

Tom Seaver: Not only are the third-baseman and the first-baseman not giving up the double, you see Pedro Guerrero on deck. Three and one the count, but the outfielders playing deep enough. Jerry White in right field, do not want to have a double here.

Enberg: Hit to centre and hit well. Dawson back and Monday will touch 'em all! Veteran Rick Monday, a home run over the centre-field fence, and the Dodgers lead two to one. And watch the Dodgers pour out of the dugout here. Two to one as Rogers, in relief, taken deep by Rick Monday. It's his day of the week.

— NBC broadcast duo of Dick Enberg and Tom Seaver chatting away on Blue Monday, October 19, 1981 (Permission: MLB Productions)

DANNY GALLAGHER'S SELECTIONS FOR SOME INTERESTING HOME RUNS HIT ON CANADIAN SOIL*

Player	Date	Venue	Opposing Pitcher	Significance
Joe Carter, Jays	Oct. 23, 1993	SkyDome, Toronto	Mitch Williams, Phillies	Won World Series
Rick Monday, Dodgers	Oct. 19, 1981	Olympic Stadium, Montreal	Steve Rogers, Expos	Won NLCS
Mike Schmidt, Phillies	Oct. 4, 1980	Olympic Stadium, Montreal	Stan Bahnsen, Expos	Clinched NL East title for Phillies
Jerry White, Expos	Oct. 16, 1981	Olympic Stadium, Montreal	Jerry Reuss, Dodgers	Won Game 3 of NLCS for Expos
Jose Canseco, A's	Oct. 7, 1989	SkyDome, Toronto	Mike Flanagan, Orioles	Helped Oakland win ALCS game[1]
Jose Bautista, Jays	Oct. 14, 2015	Rogers Centre, Toronto	Sam Dyson, Rangers	Bat flip beats Rangers for ALDS win
Edwin Encarnacion, Jays	Oct. 4, 2016	Rogers Centre, Toronto	Urbalo Jimenez, Orioles	Won AL wild card game
Willie Stargell, Pirates	May 20, 1978	Olympic Stadium, Montreal	Dale Murray, Expos	Longest Big O homer, 535 feet
Willie Stargell, Pirates	July 16, 1969	Jarry Park, Montreal	Dan McGinn, Expos	495 feet into pool beyond right field
Darryl Strawberry, Mets	April 4, 1988	Olympic Stadium, Montreal	Randy St. Claire, Expos	Hit roof rim, 525 feet[2]
Henry Rodriguez, Expos	June 15, 1997	Olympic Stadium, Montreal	Brian Moehler, Tigers	Hit roof rim, 525 feet[3]
Joe Carter, Jays	July 16, 1996	SkyDome, Toronto	John Wasdin, Athletics	First Blue Jay to hit fifth deck, 483 feet[4]
Manny Ramirez, Indians	June 3, 2001	SkyDome, Toronto	Chris Carpenter, Jays	491 feet, believed longest in Toronto
Mack Jones, Expos	April 14, 1969	Jarry Park, Montreal	Nelson Briles, Cardinals	1st MLB home run in Canada
Richie Zisk, White Sox	April 7, 1977	Exhibition Stadium, Toronto	Bill Singer, Jays	1st MLB home run in Toronto
Babe Ruth, Providence Grays	Sept. 5, 1914	Hanlan's Point, Toronto	Ellis Johnson, Maple Leafs	First pro homer for the Sultan of Swat

[1] Rickey Henderson was once quoted as saying Canseco's homer travelled 600 feet.

[2] Dave Kingman of the Mets hit the Big O's roof rim June 1, 1977, but umpire Bruce Froemming ruled it foul.

[3] Montreal-born Orioles prospect Ntema Ndungidi hit a batting-practice home run off the roof rim at the Big O in May, 1997.

[4] Toronto writer Ian Hunter believes that 20 home runs have hit the fifth deck in Toronto.

*Source: off the top of Danny Gallagher's head and online reference sites.

I never had another chance. It was disappointing. We were beat up for so long in the locker room. It took a while for reality to sink in. I was sort of numb.

We just couldn't believe it. You knew how close you had been. There was a lot of emotion. It was a tough moment in anybody's career when you're that close and don't make it. Everybody feels that by getting to the World Series, you feel like you have won, and we didn't. We were close and we didn't make it.

We lost to the Dodgers in a series that could have gone either way. The Rick Monday home run is famous in all of our minds. We lost out to three teams in 1979, '80, '81 that went on to win three different World Series. That's how close we were. With a little luck, we could have been like the Oakland Athletics (1972 to '74) or the Cincinnati Reds (1975 to '76). We could have gone down in history as one of the greatest teams and one of the biggest household names in baseball vernacular.

You look at it and say what if? I still see a pitch against Valenzuela. I don't remember the count and I didn't swing at it. It was on the outer part of the plate. It was high enough.

Did he wish he had swung at it? Parrish said, "I wish I had swung. I do. To this day, I still think of some of the pitches I saw and could I have done something with them."

Translated, maybe he should have swung instead of taking the pitches. And maybe it would have made a difference in that tight game.

Game 5 starter Ray Burris also preached that the Expos would have benefited greatly from a seven-game series, rather than the five-game set. "If we had two extra games, it would have made a difference. I truly believe we would have won a seven-game series."

Little did Parrish know that October 19, 1981, would be his last game as an Expo. Near the end of spring training in 1982, the righty-hitting Parrish was traded along with Dave Hostetler to the Texas Rangers for left-handed hitter Al Oliver. The trade was a crushing blow to him and a shock to his teammates.

Expos general manager John McHale wanted to give sophomore Tim Wallach the third-baseman's job and figured Parrish was expendable. In retrospect, Parrish was sorely missed. He was the epitome of leadership on the field and in the clubhouse. A tall, rugged, Hollywood-handsome man, he wasn't averse to critiquing players in the clubhouse with constructive or objective criticism if something needed to be said.

There's something very subtle about leadership and Parrish provided it. Gary Carter may have thought he was the Expos' leader in those days, but Parrish and Andre Dawson were exemplary, too. Parrish would go on to play five and a half seasons with the Rangers while Oliver dished out two outstanding seasons with the Expos before he departed.

> It was disappointing to be traded because the Expos were the only team I had ever known. It was a shock. I had a lot of friends on the team and in the city of Montreal.
>
> I don't feel like I could choose one teammate as being a favourite. I liked so many of those guys and respected the way they played. A few guys had good things to say after the trade. The best compliments are the ones coming from your teammates. It's always a good feeling, but having John McHale say later that it was one of his worst trades was a nice compliment after the fact.
>
> I know at the time they felt like we were a right-handed dominated team. Cromartie was the only regular left-handed hitter. He wasn't an RBI guy, but he hit for average and was a table setter. They felt like they needed a left-handed batter, so they got Oliver.

Trading Parrish just didn't make sense in the long run.

Chapter 23

Jerry White: The Final Out in Game 5

For close to 37 years, Jerry White has looked at the newspaper photo on the wall and he has viewed the YouTube video. They're both constant reminders. He sees himself almost beating out the throw at first base. Most of all, he sees himself swinging at the first pitch and he immediately feels bad.

It's the final pitch of that Game 5 of the National League Championship Series in 1981 and Bob Welch is on the mound for the Dodgers to save the game for Fernando Valenzuela, who had faltered in the bottom of the ninth.

Valenzuela retired the first two batters. Rodney Scott was out trying to get on with a bunt down the first-base line. Valenzuela fielded the ball and tossed it to first-baseman Steve Garvey. Andre Dawson then flied to right. That's when Valenzuela got into trouble. The left-handed phenom from Mexico issued two full-count bases on balls, first to Gary Carter, then to Larry Parrish, prompting Dodgers manager Tommy Lasorda to signal for Welch in the bullpen.

After witnessing White's go-ahead three-run homer from the right side against lefty Jerry Reuss in Game 3, there was no way Lasorda was going to let White stand up there and bat right against Valenzuela.

This strategy would also apply to Dodgers closer Steve Howe, who, like Valenzuela, was also a southpaw.

If Lasorda brought in his ace reliever, Howe, then White would have stayed his ground and batted right-handed. So righty-throwing Welch was on to face White. Welch had pitched the entire 1981 regular season as a starter and had a head-turning 9–5 record and a 3.44 ERA. But in the playoffs, he had been relegated to the bullpen.

Welch and Howe battled alcohol or drug abuse, but they somehow found a way to perform between the white lines. They both died way too early, Welch at 57, Howe a mere 48.

"I didn't want White hitting right-handed. I wanted to switch him around," Lasorda told reporters later.

Welch came in and threw one pitch. White swung at it and pulled it deep into the area between first base and second. Davey Lopes had played White to pull, and he was right on, so he merely shifted to his left a wee bit, gobbled the ball up, and fired it to Garvey, who fell down as he cradled the ball with an overstretch as White barely missed beating it out for the single that would have kept the rally alive.

Garvey got on his knees, hunched back, and thrust his gloved left hand and right hand in the air in that signature style of his as Welch came over to congratulate him, pulling him off the ground into a bear hug.

After watching Carter and Parrish work Valenzuela to full counts of more than five pitches, White went against conventional wisdom by going after the first pitch. Not good strategy. That's why he was kicking his ass then and still is decades later for not holding his bat back and making Welch work.

"If you fail, you get hard on yourself," White said about this play. "Oh, my, that was very disappointing. I really didn't want to hit that first pitch. I just went against my hitting plan. He threw me a sinker. I didn't want to hit it. The mind says no and the hand says yes."

In the on-deck circle as White got ready to head to the plate, someone gave him a few words of advice. "It's going to be a first-pitch fastball. Be ready," the guy told White.

The unidentified player — who it was, White doesn't actually remember — wasn't trying to tell him to swing at the first pitch, but it almost seemed that way. Years ago, White told me the person was Carter but now he's not so sure. In the on-deck circle was Warren Cromartie. White, to this day, regrets what he did.

As a pinch-hitter, a fourth outfielder, and a bench player, there was always a time for patience, but on that day, that moment, there was no patience. After swinging all day batting right-handed against the lefty Valenzuela, White switched around to bat left against Welch.

Someone told me, but I try not to remember because it should have been my own intuition as to what I had a feel for, but I'm usually taking the first pitch, getting a feel for his velocity and a feel for the catchers. I saw movement back there with the catcher, the more pitches and velocity, and I'm a better hitter with two strikes. I wanted to hit it to the opposite field. I kind of rolled the bat over. It wasn't a really good swing on the pitch.

If I'd really swung at it, it would have gone somewhere else. They probably knew I would try to pull it, so I was trying to go up the middle off of Welch. I didn't think he would challenge me with a fastball. He had good movement on his sinkerball. I was a good fastball hitter from both sides of the plate. That's where it went, down to second and I almost beat it out. I could run pretty good. I was known more as a bench guy, a pinch-hitter. I knew I was a good fastball hitter from both sides of the plate.

I wish I wouldn't have swung. I'm not a first-pitch swinger. I could work a walk. Usually, I take the first pitch. I can pretty much work the count. It's something that happens in the game, any series. I was in the game a long time, it happens. It was my decision to swing at that pitch. If I had to do it again, I'd take a different approach. It's funny, I see that picture. I'm looking at it all the time. I think of it all the time. It's in my office on the wall with a bunch of newspaper clippings. I should move it so I won't have to look at it. From that day to this day, I look at it. I think of it.

You have to get over it. I'm trying to get over it. It's failure. It's tough. Most of the time, you're failing. I sat on the bench after the game and the Dodgers were celebrating. I was thinking of what I swung at. It was real tough. We thought we were going to play the Yankees. All of our bags were packed, our wives were up in the stands.

In the next breath, White thought positive by saying, "I can say that if I didn't hit that home run in Game 3, we probably wouldn't have come to that fifth game. I was a hero and then I was a goat. I'd been a hero a couple of times in my career. Then I was a goat. But when I look at my career, I was pretty good as a hero. I pat myself on the back."

Had White ever thought of hitting right-handed against Welch instead of left because he had success against Reuss?

As far as switching around on Welch, I could not ever do it.... Switch-hitting helped me get to the big leagues and each and every game, each and every last at-bat, I either go down swinging if it's right or left I'm batting. Win or lose, I better myself the next day. I have never done that, stayed batting the same way if a new pitcher came in.

I think I may have tried it once in Triple-A, and the manager may have suggested it because we had a bunch of switch-hitters. That may be my only recollection of a situation where I didn't switch. If I didn't want to switch, I'd probably tell the manager. I had faced Valenzuela from the right side three times that game so going to the left side kind of tricks your mind to get some timing. I'd always felt better switching from the left to the right during a game.

Whatever way White feels, losing pitcher Steve Rogers doesn't think his teammate should feel the way he does about thinking he's a "goat."

"Good lord, no," Rogers said. "We won as a team and lost as a team. You know I heard Andre Dawson say he could have broken that game open in the first inning, anything in a critical moment. Everybody will look back

RAINES'S FATHER LOST OUT
ON COMPANY-PAID TRIP

Tim Raines's father Ned Sr. was one of those in the Expos family who was really hurt by Blue Monday.

"That home run by Rick Monday, that did me in," the patriarch of the Raines family recalled. "Oh man, I was so disappointed. I'll never forget it."

For good reason. Orlando area–based Hubbard Construction had employed Raines as a grader operator and supervisor for years and had promised an all-expenses paid package for him if the Expos beat the Dodgers. Trips to Montreal and New York were on the docket.

"The company promised me that on my vacation they would pay for my whole trip for the World Series," Ned Sr. said. "They were going to give me the money. That didn't pan out. They were disappointed."

Not as much as he was, though.

at what they could have done. I understand Jerry White never shirked responsibility, whatever the competitor was in him."

Said White, "I understand Steve's situation coming into a ballgame [against Rick Monday] unfamiliar with his job description and the atmosphere of the crowd. Man, it was very exciting. And an inning later, I was put in that same atmospheric situation, but it was rather normal for me because I entered my mindset for those situations during the season but with more surrounding butterflies. The only problem is that I swung at a pitch that's really not normal for me in that situation. I failed, and usually I come out on top, but I think I can honestly say I've had more success than failures in my career."

One of White's other regrets is his less than pleasant departure from the Minnesota Twins as a coach following the 2006 season, leaving him just 41 days short of a full major-league pension. The Twins had even passed White over for many years when filling out their coaching roster for each season. That meant that instead of giving White major-league service time for coaching, they would give it to someone else.

Each major-league team is allowed five coaches who qualify for service time. The other coaches don't get major-league service. They get minor-league benefits instead.

"Any time a job opening came up, the Twins would give the service time to the person coming in," White said. "I was always passed over. I was pissed off. When I was let go, the general manager, Terry Ryan, said he wanted to make changes. It wasn't that I was a bad coach or that I had done anything wrong, but it's left a bad taste in my mouth. It sucks after 43 years in the game and getting passed over. I was always passed up when new coaches came and they were chosen."

White has never been fortunate enough to get another coaching job but is thankful for all of the great memories of his time as a player and coach.

"I was voted into a hall of fame, the Caribbean Baseball Hall of Fame, and I won a batting championship playing winter ball," White said. "When I played for Dick Williams with the West Palm Beach Tropics in the Senior Professional Baseball Association in 1989, I played first base and I almost won the stolen-base title. I lost by one. It would have been the first time that a first-baseman won a stolen-base championship in any league."

Now if only we could convince White not to think too much about hitting that first pitch by Welch. *Ottawa Citizen* scribes Bob Elliott and Eddie MacCabe both wrote that bench player John Milner should have pinch-hit for White. Either Milner or White were worthy options. Even hot prospect Terry Francona.

Part Five

AFTER BLUE MONDAY: THE LONG FADE-OUT

Chapter 24

Reardon's Secret Is Out

S pring training in 2017 in Jupiter, Florida, and the picnic tables outside the Miami Marlins' clubhouse are starting to jam up with players, team officials, and media.

As I chatted with former Expos trainers Ron McClain and Mike Kozak and astute play-by-play man Dave Van Horne, a nugget was revealed about Jeff Reardon close to 40 years after the fact. A fact I didn't know about, a fact most Expos fans never realized: Reardon had lifelong back problems that may have been the reason it wasn't him pitching that famous at-bat to Rick Monday.

"What I remember is Jeff Reardon not being able to pitch," Kozak said. "He had a chronic back injury. He had conditions that he was born with. It was not a traumatic back injury. It's just that he had to manage his back."

After I prodded and asked more questions and received more information from various people, I finally went to the source; and yes, Reardon admitted he had back problems. The back issue had been around since his birth in 1955. He and the team, though, had put it around that it was a tender elbow that had been bothering him a bit on that fateful October 19. Yes, there were — and are — a lot of plots, subplots, nuances, suspense, drama, and anecdotal stuff related to those final minutes of Game 5.

Reardon was warming up in the bullpen down the right-field line with Expos ace Steve Rogers, who had sidled up to manager Jim Fanning and pitching coach Galen Cisco and volunteered to pitch in the game, if needed. The score was 1–1. Fanning was taking starter Ray Burris out of the game, much to Burris's chagrin.

"I [had] got up alongside Rogers," Reardon recollected. "I figured I was warming up and coming in if we were tied. I thought Steve was just warming up like he did for the World Series."

So just a minute or so after the conclusion of the eighth inning, Fanning came out and motioned to home-plate umpire Harry Wendelstedt that he wanted Rogers. Then Wendelstedt told first-base umpire Joe West of Fanning's intentions, but not many people in the ballpark were convinced who Fanning actually wanted. Reardon figured he was the guy.

"Joe West came down to the bullpen and put his hand on his face, motioning for the pitcher with the beard to come in. I had a beard and Steve was starting to grow one. I figured it was me. I started to walk in. I had crossed the line to cross the field. In those days, the bullpen was on the sideline past first base, not behind the home run fence in right," Reardon said.

"They don't want me?" a puzzled Reardon asked West.

"No, they want Rogers."

"Are you sure?"

"Yes, it's Rogers."

Now the stretch, and here's the 3–1 pitch. It's swung on, a fly ball to centre field. Dawson going back, at the warning track, at the wall. That ball is a home run, that ball is out of here, that is a home run for Rick Monday. The Dodgers' bench clears to congratulate Rick Monday. A two-out home run in the ninth inning. It appears Andre Dawson had room but then he ran out of room as the ball cleared the fence at about the 385 mark. A ninth-inning home run and the Dodgers have gone ahead 2–1.

— CTV play-by-play man Ron Reusch's description of Rick Monday's home run off of Steve Rogers, October 19, 1981 (Permission: MLB Productions)

1981 Expos managers and coaches

Dick Williams	Died July 7, 2011
Jim Fanning	Died April 25, 2015
Pat Mullin	Died Aug. 14, 1999
Steve Boros	Died Dec. 29, 2010
Vern Rapp	Died Dec. 31, 2015
Norm Sherry	Lives in San Diego
Galen Cisco	Lives in Celina, Ohio
Ozzie Virgil Sr.	Mets' Dominican scout

1981 Dodgers staff

Tommy Lasorda	Lives in Fullerton, Calif.
Ron Perranoski	Lives in Vero Beach, Fla.
Manny Mota	Lives in Dominican Republic
Mark Cresse	Calif. baseball school
Monty Basgall	Died Sept. 22, 2005
Danny Ozark	Died May 7, 2009

1981 NLCS umpiring personnel

Joe West	Still umping
Dutch Rennert	Died June 17, 2018
Paul Runge	Lives in San Diego
Paul Pryor	Died Dec. 15, 1995
Eric Gregg	Died June 5, 2009
Harry Wendelstedt	Died March 9, 2012

Compiled by Danny Gallagher with help from online sites.

So Reardon walked back to the bullpen disappointed and watched as Rogers trotted out to the pitcher's mound.

"I was shocked they didn't call me," Reardon said.

> Steve had never pitched in relief, except maybe once. Why they took Rogers I don't know. Why would I warm up if they didn't want me? If they didn't want me, what was I warming

up for? I was definitely ready to pitch. Oh, yeah, I could have pitched. I was psyched to go in. That's why I was warming up. I was warming up to go in the game and I thought Steve was warming up for the first game of the World Series.

Ronnie Mac told them I was all right, and I told them. It's my job to tell the manager. If I'm warming up in the game, I'm all right. But they picked Steve. He was the best pitcher. I was a young pitcher and Steve was the veteran. I was told after that Rick Monday had struck out four times against me before that game.

The official company line at the time was that Fanning and general manager John McHale didn't want Reardon to aggravate his elbow injury and that any back woes Reardon might have had were not part of the equation.

"After one of the games in Los Angeles, I felt a twinge in the elbow. I had a little soreness in the elbow but the trainers did some work on it and it was okay," Reardon said.

"Reardon was perfectly able to go that day but the powers-that-be said otherwise," McClain told me. "They wanted him to wait another day, but there wasn't another day."

There are so many myths, fictions, and other various theories about Reardon and his injuries. In an account of the Blue Monday game in the *Montreal Gazette*, Fanning made it known that indeed Reardon would have been used in a certain scenario if Burris faltered.

"If we replaced Burris during an inning, we would have used Reardon, but if we replaced him after an inning, then we would have brought in Rogers," Fanning said.

In the mystique surrounding that final game and why Rogers was used instead of Reardon, there was yet another factor. It is now known that Fanning told confidantes shortly after the game that he was "spooked" by the fact Reardon had been roughed up by the Dodgers in Game 1 in Los Angeles.

The highly regarded retrosheet.org website preserves the story of that game: Reardon came in in the eighth, in relief of Bill Gullickson with the Dodgers leading 2–0. After retiring the first two batters, Reardon gave up a two-run homer to Pedro Guerrero and a solo shot to Mike Scioscia. The Dodgers won 5–1 to take the first game of the series.

Reardon had saved the first two games of the Phillies series but was the losing pitcher in Game 4. The score was tied 5–5 when little-known and rarely used George Vukovich hit a pinch-hit walk-off homer in the 10th inning to beat the Expos 6–5 and force a fifth and deciding game. (It is still the only walk-off homer in Phillies playoff history.)

What was quite remarkable, though, about Reardon's stint just prior to Vukovich's home run was that he had retired the first eight batters he faced. That piece of art was, remember, in the days when closers did more than just pitch the ninth inning. But it was undeniably true that in two consecutive games he had pitched, Reardon had given up three homers; so Fanning had every right to be a little concerned about him.

As it turned out, Reardon wasn't used in the last four games of the NLDS, although in two of those games Rogers and Ray Burris had complete outings. It should also be mentioned that in Game 4, won 7–1 by the Dodgers, Fryman had been nailed for three hits and three runs in the eighth inning in what had been a 1–1 nail-biter until then.

In one report in the *Montreal Gazette* on October 15, four days before Game 5, Reardon was quoted as saying he visited a doctor about stiffness in his arm and he was told by the doctor that he risked injury by pitching.

"Naw, I had no back problems that game. I don't know what their thinking was. People assume it was my back. It wasn't my back," Reardon told me in 2017.

Funny thing: as much as Reardon and other people have since brushed off his back woes, *New York Times* sports reporter Joseph Durso mentioned the issue in his story two days *before* Game 5. "And the Expos conceded that their star relief pitcher Jeff Reardon was suffering from a strained muscle in his back and might not be available for a few days," Durso wrote.

"All of this stuff about me not being available is not true," Reardon told me. "All of this stuff saying I wasn't available was something I found out after the fact. But I told the Expos I was ready for Game 5. I had a strained muscle, but it wasn't in my back, it was in my arm. I had a bad back every time I pitched."

That's true. Truth of the matter is that Reardon was born in Dalton, Massachusetts, on October 1, 1955, with back problems. Something officially called spondylolisthesis.

"To this day, he has back problems," Dave Van Horne told me. And Reardon told me,

> I was born with a curvature of the spine that prevents flexibility. I could never even touch my toes. When I came to the Expos, the first thing Bill Lee said was, "This guy can't touch his toes but he can throw 100 miles per hour." I was young then, so the back wasn't so bad, but later I had to have surgery a few times.
>
> When I went to Montreal, the trainers decided to work on me in the fourth inning and stretch the back. That was a ritual with the trainers the rest of my career for another 13 years. The first three innings of a game, I'd sit in the dugout. Then the next three innings, I'd go to the clubhouse and they'd massage me. With the media around, we couldn't do it before a game. Then I'd go to the bullpen for the last three innings. They'd do 15 minutes of deep tissue rub on my lower back. They'd dig their thumbs in there. It wouldn't feel right but I got up from the table and felt great. It kept me going. There were times when I could hardly move before they worked on me.

"We'd give him treatment every day; ice, massages, the whirlpool," McClain said.

"I've had two operations on my back in the last seven years," Reardon told me. "Dr. David Campbell at the Florida Spine Centre in Jupiter has done the operations. He's done hundreds of surgeries over the years. It's kind of risky getting the operation, but a few years ago I had to use a walker and I said, 'I can't live like that.' I couldn't walk very far. I was pretty upset about that, but now I've got to the point where I'm walking three or four miles a day."

Chapter 25

Bronfman and Others
on Choosing Rogers

J ust like any regular fan, Charles Bronfman was sitting near the Expos' dugout on the first-base side for Game 5, not in the executive suite, where he might have benefited from the warmth on that cold day.

He was watching when, with the score tied 1–1, Jim Fanning decided to go with a clean slate to start the ninth and summoned Steve Rogers.

"I was surprised," Bronfman told me 36 years later, about the decision to bring Rogers in. "He had won a game earlier in the series and he won two games against Philadelphia. He pitched like hell in both games against Philadelphia. He was our best pitcher." In the next breath, though, Bronfman added, "The problem was that we were tied 1–1."

Good point. Bronfman, like many others studying Fanning's strategy, was wondering why Rogers was brought in when the game was tied, perhaps thinking that it would have been better to hold Rogers back to save the game if the Expos got ahead. Said Bronfman,

> I was told Jeff Reardon had arm or shoulder problems.
> Jim had huge faith in Steve Rogers. You know, you make

the decision. You're either a hero or a bum. Had he struck out Monday, or if he hadn't hit the home run, things would have been different. Monday just got lucky. What dings me off is that I thought Steve threw Monday a good pitch. At one of those exhibition games the Blue Jays had at Olympic Stadium a few years ago, I ran into Steve near an elevator and I told him that it was a good pitch. He said, "No, it was not a good pitch. It was up too much."

My only regret in baseball is not being in the World Series. Oh, for sure, I thought we were going to win the Dodgers series after we split in Los Angeles. If it weren't for the Dodgers, we would have beaten the Yankees. Oh, yeah. You know, Blue Monday took us away from the World Series. That loss no doubt is the biggest disappointment of my time as owner.

Bronfman would wear his heart on his sleeve for 23 seasons, but never more than in October 1981. He was in New York at Shea Stadium when Wallace Johnson hit that two-run triple to help the Expos clinch a playoff berth for the first time in franchise history.

When the Expos took the series to five games against Philadelphia in the NLDS, this heir to the Seagram empire attended every one. When the Expos went the maximum five games against Los Angeles in the NLCS, Bronfman again attended every one, as did Dodgers owner Peter O'Malley, who sat behind the Dodgers' dugout on the third-base side, silent and clenching his fists. On that cold day in Montreal for Game 5, O'Malley, like Bronfman, could have sat in the warmth of the press box in a suite, but there he was in the stands. When Monday hit the home run, O'Malley at first couldn't believe that it had happened. He wasn't convinced even when Monday thrust his arm in the air after rounding first base.

"It was unbelievable. Until we saw him go around second waving his arm, then we knew. By golly, it went out," O'Malley recalled.

As he made his way out of the stadium to head to the Dodgers' clubhouse, who should O'Malley meet along the way but two familiar Expos executives.

What I really remember like it was yesterday was leaving the stadium. We ran into Charles Bronfman and John McHale, two people I really admired.... They were coming from near the Expos side. They were first-class. They always did the right thing for baseball.

Our win hurt that franchise. I felt really sad seeing that happen. That's what was really sad about that. You think of the guy who loses. We had hurt the franchise and I was not happy about that. I knew they were stunned. At least, I think they were stunned.

If Montreal could have won, it would have helped the franchise. They offered congratulations and they were very gracious, extremely gracious. I've always had fond memories of the Expos and Montreal. Jackie Robinson played for us there for our farm team in Triple-A and manager Tommy Lasorda played there for the Royals.

"I think what Peter O'Malley was trying to say was that it would be nice if you could have two winners and no losers," Bronfman said. "I felt bad for Steve. I remember running into Bobby Thomson, who hit the home run for the New York Giants to beat the Brooklyn Dodgers in that playoff game in 1951. Bobby came to a game at Jarry Park. He was a salesman for a trucking company. I said, 'Bobby, you're a nice man. Why do such a terrible thing?'"

Said Rogers, "It [the Monday homer] wasn't like the Bobby Thomson homer off Ralph Branca, but for Montreal and Canada, it was the equivalent."

Another man pivotal in that ninth inning was Expos pitching coach Galen Cisco, one of Fanning's top lieutenants and a man who went reluctantly along with Fanning's decision to replace Burris with Rogers and not Reardon.

"That was one of those damned-if-you-do, damned-if-you-don't situations," Cisco told me. "Monday hit the home run. I remember it like it was yesterday. If Jim had had a second chance, he would have left Burris in. Ray had done his job, so Jim thought he would close the game with our short-game guys in the bullpen. Here's my thought on this: Steve hadn't pitched in relief all year. It was a different situation for him. The game is on the line. Everything is on the line. I thought he would get Monday out, but he didn't. I don't know how strong Reardon's arm was. Reardon might have said he was fine, but in Jim's mind he just didn't want to bring in a guy who was not a hundred percent."

Cisco brought up a similar situation that had happened when he was pitching coach of the Kansas City Royals in the final game of the 1977 American League Championship Series against the Yankees. Just as in Game 5 for the Expos against the Dodgers when Rogers came on, Royals manager Whitey Herzog, with backing from Cisco, brought starting pitcher Dennis Leonard into a tight game in the top of the ninth at Royals Stadium.

In this particular case, unlike the 1–1 tie in 1981, Leonard was trying to save a 3–2 Kansas City lead. Leonard was the fourth Kansas City pitcher that game. Paul Blair blooped a single to centre to start the inning and Leonard walked Roy White. At that point, with men on first and second, Leonard was taken out and replaced. The Yankees came back to stun the Royals 5–3 to advance to the World Series, where they beat the Dodgers. Just as with Rogers in 1981, Leonard was the losing pitcher.

"We brought Leonard in to the game in the very same situation and it didn't work that time either. Blair blooped a hit and it just cleared the infield and it was short of the outfield. After that situation, with Steve in 1981, I didn't like that idea," Cisco said, of bringing in a starting pitcher in relief. "Steve was our best pitcher. He was the best guy to close it out. He just made one bad pitch. As a sinkerball pitcher, Rogers always tried to keep the ball down. Monday was a low-ball hitter."

But Rogers got the pitch up. When Cisco was told that Rogers said his heart was beating very fast in that ninth inning, he quipped, "My heart used to be like that every game."

Dodgers first-baseman Steve Garvey hadn't been too confident coming back to Montreal from Los Angeles after Game 4. "Ray Burris had pitched great in the second game in Los Angeles, so that put us in jeopardy," he said. "It was tough. We had to go there, to Montreal, and get it done. They went ahead 2–1 in the series and then in the fourth game, it was close for quite a while and then I hit a home run to give us some breathing room.

THE BLUE MONDAY HOMER:
REASONS AND SCENARIOS

- Starter Steve Rogers volunteered to pitch in relief.
- Lefties Woodie Fryman and Bill Lee were available.
- With a roof, there would have been no Blue Monday.
- Dick Williams wouldn't have used Rogers in relief.
- Closer Jeff Reardon had a tender elbow but was cleared to pitch.
- Jim Fanning was spooked by recent HRs Reardon coughed up.
- Management was concerned about Reardon's apparent back woes.
- Youppi! was too consumed with bothering the Dodgers.

So that brought it to one shot, one game to see who would go to the World Series. It was a close game where we thought we would have to manufacture a run, and as the day went on, it got colder and colder. We thought there might be snow. But we got a home run. Rick had good backswing and the ball carried over the fence."

The celebration was under way. Monday was the focus of attention as teammates, Lasorda, and the other coaches swarmed him. In the clubhouse, Monday was doused with some bubbly. "It was very cold, and it was a round bottle. That's all I know," Monday said. "I don't know the name. Did it ever taste good, but it was also the worst-tasting drink."

Later, out in the parking lot, as the Dodgers prepared to board a bus for the airport, outfielder Dusty Baker got embroiled in a dustup with some Expos fans. The result wasn't good for the team. "These guys were messing with some of our wives," Baker told me. "I got into a fight. I hurt my right hand. I never let on."

Baker shook his head when I asked if reporters knew about the injury. He went up to Lasorda and told him. Then it was on to New York, but not before some celebrating on the plane. "We had a very enjoyable flight to New York of an hour and fifteen minutes," Monday said. "Celebrations at thirty-thousand feet are very enjoyable. It was a very joyous flight. We celebrated from Montreal to New York. We got in fairly late. Tommy Lasorda and I were up early the next morning to go on the NBC News's *Today* show with Bryant Gumbel."

As the camera swung to Gumbel for his lead-in, he welcomed Monday and Lasorda, showing them the front page of the *New York Daily News* with the banner headline "Monday, Monday" in about 80-point type. Yes, "Monday, Monday," alluding to that famous song by the Mamas & the Papas.

"Let's turn our attention to Rick Monday, the hero," Gumbel said. "Rick, safe to say that's your biggest hit. When you came up there with two out in the ninth inning, were you looking for a pitch to put over the wall?"

"No, actually I wasn't, not with Steve Rogers out there. I had fouled back the first pitch and I wasn't expecting to see another pitch like that," Monday said.

The Dodgers went on to win the World Series that year, beating the Yankees in yet another comeback. That year the Dodgers fell behind in all three of their post-season series, only to come back and win each time. They beat the Astros, Expos, and Yankees. The Yankees took a 2–0 lead in New York but the Comeback Kids won four straight, including the clincher at Yankee Stadium.

Ironically, Pedro Guerrero, who had slumped in the series against the Expos, became a star in the World Series, going 7-for-21 with two homers and seven RBI, earning co-MVP honours along with Ron Cey and Steve Yeager.

Baker, for the record, played in each of the six games in the World Series, but his bad hand played havoc with most of his swings. He went only 4-for-24, although two of the hits came in the clincher in Game 6.

So, finally, in their fourth try at winning a World Series, the Dodgers Fab Four infield of Garvey, second-baseman Davey Lopes, shortstop Bill Russell, and third sacker Cey found glory. They had played together since June 1973, believed to be the longest-running, most stable infield quartet in baseball history.

"What we did was eliminate the memories of not winning the World Series in 1974, 1977, and 1978," Garvey said. "What you have to re-member, too, is there was no off-day between the end of our series with Montreal and the start of the World Series in New York. We lost the first two games in New York and that put us in a tough spot. But we came back and won the World Series. That stretch of time in baseball in the 1970s and part of the 1980s was what I like to call the Golden Era, that stretch from 1970 to 1985. Those were great years with some great players."

"These guys were a very special group," said long-time Dodgers public-relations specialist Steve Brener. "They battled to the bitter end in all three series. Tommy Lasorda was the master at motivation and these guys never gave up and he wouldn't let them give up. It was an unbelievable season to say the least."

For a guy from Mexico, Fernando Valenzuela could have been intimidated by the slashing cold in Montreal on October 19, but he wasn't. Dodgers owner Peter O'Malley said Valenzuela "never blinked" because he was a "young and healthy" stud of almost 20.

"Fernando didn't start opening day in April," O'Malley said. "Jerry Reuss was supposed to be the starter but he had a muscle pull or something and they went to Fernando and said, 'You're the man.' Then he went out and won eight straight games. Fernandomania took over Los Angeles, then California, and then the country. We had Fernandomania, then Nomomania (Hideo Nomo) and Chanhomania (Chan Ho Park)."

But none of the others could beat Fernandomania.

Chapter 26

Bill Lee Opens Up

Bill "Spaceman" Lee's position on what happened late in the game on Blue Monday is simple: he should have been called in to face Rick Monday.

It would have been a perfect situational matchup. You go with the percentages: lefty-throwing Lee in against lefty-swinging Monday. Rogers had retired the first two batters — Steve Garvey and Ron Cey — and Lee figures manager Jim Fanning should have brought him in to confront Monday, the third batter. Woodie Fryman, another lefty, was also available, but he was ailing.

When I sat down with Lee and his wife, Diana, over breakfast at the Sunflower Café in Springfield, New York, not far from Cooperstown, in late July of 2017, Lee told me,

> Rogers had trouble warming up. He had nothing. I knew he wasn't ready. He couldn't get loose. It wasn't Rogers's fault. He was a gutsy guy. When you throw a sinkerball like him, you throw it a little slower so it has more movement. He threw harder than he had to. Rogers gagged on it. If

Bill Lee poses here at the Sunflower Café in Springfield, NY, with his Calgary-born wife Diana.

you throw a natural sinkerball slower, he probably gets Monday to hit the ball to left field and there would be no home run. When you're trying to overthrow a pitch, you gag on it. Rogers almost gave up three home runs in that inning. He gave up the home run to Monday, but Ron Cey almost hit one out in his at-bat before Monday. Then Monday had a good swing early in the count against Rogers and just missed it a bit. He fouled it off.

Woodie was exhausted. His arm was ready to fall off. I got up to warm up on my own as soon as Monday was in the on-deck circle. I was getting warmed up to be ready for Monday. I tipped my hat to Fanning to say that I was ready, but he didn't bring me in. And the rest is history. We lose it on Fanning's desire to leave Rogers in.

When the players entered the clubhouse after the numbing loss, did anybody scream, "What was Fanning doing?"

Lee shook his head. Nobody brought up Fanning. It was more just numbness. Shock. And more shock.

It was such an unexpected loss. We should have won the World Series. If Rogers had not been pitching there, the World Series would have had a totally different outcome.

Rogers beat Steve Carlton in Philadelphia twice, so we thought we were going to go all the way. It was a very tumultuous year for me. I think that was the year I fell out of a two-storey apartment building on Marcel St. in Notre-Dame-de-Grâce in Montreal. I spent 30 days on the disabled list. And I got divorced from Miss Alaska, Mary Lou Helfrich, on December 31.

Lee said he has forgiven or has tried to forgive Fanning for allowing Rogers to pitch to Monday. Lee says he has also forgiven or tried to forgive Fanning for his role in Lee's dramatic release from the club on May 9, 1982, after which he was never to play another major-league game. But this forgiveness didn't stop Lee from flogging his former manager in public. For years, it was almost boring to hear Lee keep on about Fanning. When I reintroduced myself to Lee at the ExposFest fan festival in Montreal in April 2017, he muttered "Fanning" during our brief exchange as we walked down a hallway. I hadn't even brought up Fanning at that point.

Over the breakfast in Springfield, I asked him if he had gotten along with Fanning from the time Lee joined the Expos in 1978 to the time Fanning became manager in September 1981.

Lee nodded but didn't elaborate. "I got along with Zimmer, too," Lee said, referring to Don Zimmer, his manager most of his time with the Red Sox.

Zimmer was fine as a coach, but when they put him on the bench, there was a lot of gambling going on in games. It was Procter & Gamble. It was the rocky relationship I had with [Expos general manager] John McHale. He was a Notre Dame guy and I was a University of Southern California guy. Notre Dame didn't win much, but we did at USC. After we lost our first three games under Fanning, we called a team meeting without Fanning. I said to the players, "You disliked Dick Williams because he was a stern, tough guy, so do you want Fanning?"

I was shocked when they hired Fanning. You never bring in a front-office guy. It's the kiss of death. You let Galen Cisco or one of the other coaches take over.

When teammate Rodney Scott was released on May 8, 1982, the resulting drama marked the end of Lee's big-league career. "I wanted to kill Fanning," Lee told me later, in the 1990s. "I left Fanning a note letting him know that I didn't appreciate the manner in which he buried Rodney."

So even though there was a game on that day, again with the Dodgers, Lee protested by tearing up his uniform, leaving Olympic Stadium, and going for five Molson Export beers at Brasserie 77 with *Montreal Gazette* cartoonist Aislin (Terry Mosher). Lee skipped much of the Dodgers game before returning to the ballpark. He asked for a new uniform, but equipment manager John Silverman refused. Fanning and others had been looking for Lee so they could use him in the game, but he had been nowhere to be found. Fanning and some of his fellow coaches were full of umbrage.

"Lee keeps bringing that incident up," Fanning said more than 20 years ago. "He's obsessed with that. He gives me too much credit by saying I released him. He flatters me by saying that, but it was a unanimous decision by me, the coaches, and John McHale that he go. It's sad and unfortunate that a professional athlete would do what he did. There have been accusations by him that we blackballed him. That's wrong because none of the other teams called me or John McHale about him. You think of the coaches at the time when that happened. One coach came up to me and said, 'If you don't get rid of that SOB, I'm going to walk off this club tomorrow.'"

The one coach who could have been most disturbed by Lee's shenanigans was pitching coach Galen Cisco. Of course, bullpen coach Bob Gebhard could have been upset, too. But — surprise, surprise — Cisco wasn't the coach who demanded Lee be released. Cisco was actually quite sympathetic to Lee. The day following Lee's exit, Cisco made his way to Lee's apartment in downtown Montreal, knocked on the door, and expressed his sympathy as Lee dealt with the ignominy. There was guilt, shame, quasi-depression, shock, and a red face.

Lee has come to appreciate Cisco's gesture more and more as the years have gone by. And it's a secret Cisco is finally talking about after more than 35 years. "I don't know the whole story about Bill getting let go," Cisco told me in 2017. "Bill did some strange things. He got ahead of himself. He got caught up in something and they decided to let him go. When he got released, I made a trip to where he lived. He had gone from the ballpark. I didn't see him in the clubhouse. He was gone. He was not in uniform. I told him I was sorry to see him go. I thanked him for all of what he did. Bill was a heckuva teammate. He kept guys loose. He has thanked me on different occasions for what I did."

How did the termination go down? Before the May 9th game, early in the afternoon, McHale called Lee into his office in the company of player representative Steve Rogers and assistant general manager Gene Kirby. Lee sat down on the floor, munching on a sandwich. McHale released Lee and fined him $5,000.

"Bill [Lee] and Rodney [Scott] were pretty much glued to the hip as far as being cool, calm, and collected," teammate Jerry White said. "They added a lot of humour to the clubhouse ... so getting rid of Rodney was a blow to the team."

As history books show, Lee pitched in his last game May 7, a three-inning effort against the Dodgers. He even struck out Monday along the way. A crowd of 32,219 was on hand.

"I expected a fine ... a three-game suspension or something," Lee said in the 1990s about his release. "What I couldn't understand was getting released and getting fined, too. Why kill a guy by taking money out of his pocket?"

Said Scott in 2016, "I always appreciated Bill for standing up for me. I loved Bill. I have a lot of respect for him."

Even worse than getting released was the sinister development that Lee, at the relatively young age of 35, was never signed by another big-league club. He had a rubber arm and could pitch almost every day out of the bullpen. He was a very serviceable, low-maintenance pitcher, even though he had suffered an arm injury in a Red Sox brawl with the Yankees in 1976.

"I couldn't understand it because I was too valuable a player," Lee said in 1996. "I was a left-hander, I could start, I could relieve, I threw strikes, I ran pretty good, and I was a good hitter. I was blackballed. I was surprised. The other teams colluded against me. I was a white Satchel Paige."

Satchel Paige was one of baseball's greatest pitchers, but he never got to pitch in the majors until age 42 because of the game's racial barrier. Jackie Robinson of the Brooklyn Dodgers was chosen as the first player to break the racial barrier, in 1947, but Paige really should have been the guy. For years, baseball's white establishment of team owners refused such involvement of black players in the game.

More than 20 years later, as we sat at the Sunflower Café, Lee told me, "I had an ERA of 2.78. I told McHale there were a lot of teams who could use me. To which McHale replied, 'Don't count on it.'"

Indeed, Lee never did play another big-league game. Almost immediately after being released by the Expos, Lee put his resumé together and fired it off to the other major-league teams. One reply came back, and that was from Pittsburgh Pirates general manager Harding Peterson. As Lee puts it, Peterson replied this way: "We have enough problems without having you on the team."

Lee told me he did have a tryout of some sort with the San Diego Padres at spring training in 1984 in Yuma, Arizona. He showed up to throw under the watchful eye of general manager Jack McKeon and president Ballard Smith, who had connections to the McDonald's empire because he was married to founder Ray Kroc's daughter Linda and sat on the McDonald's board of directors.

"I got my revenge," Lee told me, as his wife Diana listened. "Revenge" on baseball for blackballing him. Lee was just getting going on telling me how he got a bagful of his own poop and threw it over a fence in the parking lot of a McDonald's eatery, when Diana intervened to stop him. So we will leave it at that.

When I brought up Lee's possible blackballing with former MLBPA executive director Don Fehr, he said, "I did find it odd. Could we have legally done something about it? I'm not sure. Careers end sometimes."

Speaking of revenge, Lee told me, "If you seek revenge, you dig two graves. A light went off in my head. I saw a light in the tunnel and realized it was a train. Same with Fanning, Zimmer, and Red Sox general manager Haywood Sullivan. A light went off in their heads. They're all on the wrong side of the wall." The spiritual wall, he meant.

Lee and Fanning had a cordial chat back in 1990 and the two met again at the 1981 Expos team reunion in Montreal in 2012. Lee also revealed to me, at the Sunflower over breakfast, that Fanning's wife Marie sent him a nice letter after Fanning's death in April 2015.

Lee also divulged for the first time his involvement in the firing of Billy Martin as manager of the Texas Rangers in 1975.

For whatever reason, Martin disliked Lee so much that he sent two dead mackerel to Lee in the Red Sox clubhouse while the Sox were visiting for a three-game series.

Coming from Martin, who was of Italian and Portuguese descent, the "gift" of dead mackerel was a mobster signal: "You're dead."

Scary stuff. Lee reported the incident and Martin was canned. Lee was delighted. "I got Billy Martin fired from Texas," Lee bellowed, as Sunflower patrons looked up and took notice.

Martin was replaced by Frank Lucchesi, one of Martin's coaches. There were reports that owner Brad Corbett and Martin had a confrontation about Lee, and Martin apparently said, "You know as much about baseball as I do about piping," referring to Corbett's background in the pipe business.

Martin and Corbett decided to keep the whole Lee issue from the media at the time. Lee didn't pitch in the Red Sox-Rangers series anyway, so that should not have been a tipping point for Martin to issue his implied threat.

Over the years, the mystery about just how Lee was injured in Montreal in the early 1980s has reached somewhat mythic proportions. At the time, he told reporters that he had been hit by a taxi after tripping to avoid a cat while he was jogging one Sunday morning before a game. But over the years, the story changed. He is now saying he fell out of a window. "It's a long story," was all Lee said, when I asked him how it happened.

"That was the second explanation of what he said had happened to him," recalled long-time Expos athletic trainer Ron McClain. "He initially came into the training room limping and holding his side. He was obviously hurt and in pain. The doctor was there and we examined him and we got a clubhouse attendant to take him to the Queen Elizabeth Hospital. Bill told us he was jogging early in the morning when a cat jumped out from under a car and startled him so bad he tripped and fell into the path of a passing taxi. He really said this. That was the official story he told us."

McClain said Lee also told him that the taxi driver helped him into the car and gave him a ride to Olympic Stadium. When he was taken to hospital, the injuries were severe. "He was diagnosed with fractured ribs and other internal injuries," McClain disclosed.

> He had internal bleeding from his spleen, I think, maybe his kidneys. He didn't really recover from this incident until the off-season.
>
> I'm not sure which story was true. Probably the second one. But when someone tells you they were hit by a cab, though, what can you say? We took it as the truth, but one never knows. The part about jumping onto a trestle and having it fall away from the building, causing him to land on a wrought iron fence was divulged the following year. As medical professionals, it really didn't matter to us. We just wanted to know where he was injured and treat that, get him healthy and back to the field when possible. This was serious. He was lucky he had no real lasting injuries.

Despite his dénouement in 1982, Lee is a baseball legend. He is one of the all-time favourite Red Sox players and one of the all-time favourite Expos. How many people can say they had a movie made about them? *Spaceman*, a 90-minute comedic drama, was released in 2016. The role of Lee was played by American actor Josh Duhamel. Lee has also been a fixture for years on Mitch Melnick's late-afternoon radio show on TSN 690 in Montreal.

Many people view Lee as eccentric and one to make bombastic, peculiar statements, but really, he displays a range of intellect; has an advanced education; and likes to discuss science, physics, and spirituality.

And he's known for being stubborn. He resented, questioned, openly defied, and confronted authority. Patience is not one of Lee's virtues, except if he's dealing with autograph seekers.

Even the notion that he warmed up on his own without authorization from Fanning or pitching coach Galen Cisco in Game 5 could be construed as Lee defying authority, but it was more likely that he was just showing initiative. He didn't need to be told to warm up. He decided on his own to warm up. He was sending a message to Fanning: you need to get me in there to face Monday.

Years ago, Lee was referred to as a flake. Some thought him a buffoon, but to this day he is a star in his own right.

To the surprise of nobody, Lee was the party-man leader during his time in Montreal.

"That '81 Expos team was mostly outlaws and renegades like the Phillies," umpire Joe West said. "They had a distinct personality with all kinds of characters. The travelling secretary, Peter Durso, is still going to court for some of the shit they pulled."

And West would know, because over the years many umpires routinely mingled with players and members of the media in bars and played cards with them — even for money at times.

Lee was a larger-than-life character when it came to playing off the field, too, and he was the ringleader for any antics in Montreal, at places such as the Sir Winston Churchill Pub, or out on the road.

"That club was sort of like a throwback club," Larry Parrish said. "There were a lot of good players who had a lot of good times away from the field. A crazy, wild guy like Bill Lee took pressure off everyone else. My goodness, you didn't have to worry too much with Bill Lee around. He was always doing something wild. That was in the days when there [were] no cellphones to record things."

Players such as Rodney Scott would get in trouble with the law while in Montreal and they'd spend some time in jail before being let go when the police found out they were Expos players. They were given leeway. Lee, Scott, Rowland Office, Ellis Valentine, and Stan Bahnsen headed the list of party animals.

"They all liked to have a good time, not with drugs, but beer and booze mostly," recalled trainer Ron McClain. "The renegades were Rodney, Rowland, Lee, and Ellis somewhat, although he was liked by most umps and people all over. Stan was a big partier."

Married players like Jerry White and Andre Dawson would opt for eateries like the Bar-B Barn on Guy Street or Big Sly's near the old Montreal Forum, which was run by a Barbadian woman. It was heaven for anyone who loved West Indian and Dominican food. "Big Sly's was our quick-to-go-to restaurant. We hung out there, especially on Sundays," White said.

Lee, Scott, and several others were known to have smoked marijuana and some players would even utilize hallways near the clubhouse and field at Olympic Stadium to roll their joints on towels spread on the cement floor. But something even more serious came later: cocaine.

"It was definitely a problem. I can't speak for anybody, though," Parrish said of cocaine use among the Expos.

"Cocaine was just on fire in the industry. It was terrible," said one man who spoke to me off the record. "I actually confronted a few guys. I threw a couple of guys on the ground. I'd say 'What the hell are you doing?' I was fairly aggressive about going after players. Cocaine was a wild firestorm. It was the rage among the players and in the entertainment industry. It was the party drug. You could make an all-star team of the people using it. People were not getting the message. The union wouldn't do anything. The owners were just winking at it because some players were so good that the owners would just forget about the problem. This is very confidential. This is way off the record."

Back in the 1980s, Cardinals manager Whitey Herzog told the *Washington Post* that 11 of his players were "heavy users" of cocaine. "It got so bad that when we went to Montreal, which was where they all seemed to get it, I had to have us fly in on the day of the game. That way, I knew we'd play decent for one night, even though the rest of the trip might be a lost cause."

Herzog claimed that a player for the Expos was one of the "biggest dealers in the league. He ruined his own talent, but teams just keep giving him chances. He's still playing." He did not identify the player, but it's believed that he was referring to Valentine.

Almost every important Herzog trade after 1980 unloaded one of his confessed, rehabilitated, or suspected cocaine abusers.

His managerial problems with cocaine use among players go back to his years in Kansas City in the late 1970s, the *Post* article stated.

"I'll always be convinced that cocaine cost me a world title with the Royals," Herzog said. "These guys are so rich they can afford any amount of drugs. Once they start, they can't stop until it's gone."

Chapter 27

An Eventful Season
for Francona

W as the Expos' failure to gain a berth in the 1981 World Series the biggest disappointment of Terry Francona's career as a player? "Oh boy," he said, pausing. "Naw, I don't think so. I was naive then, 21, 22 years old. You thought you would win every year. My biggest disappointment was when I got hurt. My career was taken away from me. I couldn't play [after] I got hurt. It was disappointing not being able to play."

Francona's foot caught on the turf during a game in 1982 and he wrecked his right knee. Then he wrecked his left knee during a game in 1984. He was never the same afterward and couldn't revive his career. He has had both knees replaced since.

Francona was a highly touted player at the University of Arizona in Tucson, and before you could say Jack Robinson he was in the majors playing for the Expos.

"I mean, things were going so fast," Francona said.

This is how fast it went. This hitting machine batted .401 with a phenomenal 84 RBI in the spring of 1980 at Arizona, where he helped the Wildcats to the College World Series. He was voted the winner of the

Golden Spikes Award, which is given to the best amateur baseball player in the United States, and he was selected as the most outstanding player in the College World Series.

That was just shortly before he was selected by the Expos in the first round of the June 1980 amateur free-agent draft. He finished out that season with the Double-A Memphis Chicks, batting .300, with a homer and 18 RBI.

"When we got Francona, we sent him right to Double-A. He didn't play rookie ball or Single-A," recalled Bob Gebhard, the Expos' farm director. "I remember him as a guy who worked extremely hard and was always in the game. He knew how to play the game. He always hit for a big average. He didn't hit for power. He'd hit line drives, hardly ever struck out, and hardly ever walked.

"I remember going to Memphis [on] a lot of trips to see him. I remember Jim Fanning being frustrated because he thought Francona should hit for more power. But he was a good enough player and hitter. He didn't have great speed, but he ran smartly."

Francona continued his torrid pace in '81 as he worked his way up through the Expos' minor-league system. Ironically, he was never a power hitter, as Gebhard noted, but boy could he hit. With combined figures from Double-A Memphis and Triple-A Denver, Francona was batting .351 with 76 RBI when he was promoted by the Expos on August 19.

"My feet never touched the ground," Francona said. "I was trying to take everything in. They were in the middle of a pennant race. It was my Triple-A trainer at Denver who called me early that morning and said to get a plane to Houston. I was shocked at the call. That was in the days before the internet. I got to the ballpark in the fifth inning and I went into the game as a pinch-hitter in the eighth inning. I was all geared up to face Nolan Ryan and then they brought in Dave Smith, who threw me curveballs." Francona grounded out to first unassisted.

"We had a lot of veteran players who were so good to the younger players," Francona said. "People like Steve Rogers, Larry Parrish, Andre Dawson, Chris Speier. They taught you to treat the game respectfully and professionally. It was so exciting, and it was fun."

In what must be some sort of professional baseball record, or close to it, Francona played in 168 regular-season games in 1981: 41 with Memphis,

Terry Francona entertains the media after a World Series game in 2016.

93 with Denver, and 34 with the Expos. Given that Major League Baseball has a 162-game slate, that was some accomplishment. No wonder Francona said life was going "so fast" that year.

In the space of six weeks following his promotion, the kid from New Easton, Pennsylvania, was tasting a berth in the playoffs when pinch-hitter Wallace Johnson hit that two-run triple at Shea Stadium to help the Expos club get its first taste of post-season play.

In the National League Division Series against the Phillies, Francona did his part by going 4-for-12. Francona was kept on the roster for the Dodgers series and made two appearances. He pinch-hit for Bill Gullickson in Game One in the eighth inning and struck out, and he was a defensive replacement for Tim Raines in Game Two in the ninth inning.

"Three of my hits in that Philadelphia series were bunts," Francona said, chuckling. "Mike Schmidt was playing back at third, so I bunted. Steve Rogers was on another planet in that series. He was hot."

What does he remember about the Monday home run that sunk the Expos?

"When he hit it, your heart dropped," Francona said. "Andre Dawson went back. It kind of kicks you in the stomach."

What if? That's a question that has gone through Francona's mind over the years. What if he had stayed healthy? Would he have been a star player like he was in the minors and at the University of Arizona?

To make up for that missed trip to the World Series in 1981, Francona years later became a superb major-league manager. He won two World Series as skipper of the Red Sox and came close again in 2016 when the Indians bowed to the Cubs in Game 7.

Chapter 28

Don't Blame Rogers

t's easy to use Rogers as a scapegoat for the Expos' loss in that final game of the NLCS, but that's not the way it should work. You have to blame the team as a whole.

"We win as a team, we lose as a team," Rogers told me, as he's told many others in interviews over the years when he's asked what happened.

Just think that in three of the five games against the Dodgers, all losses, the Expos scored only one run. They scored a total of only 10 runs in five games. Not good. Get the message?

Individual players were not playing up to snuff. Andre Dawson was 3-for-20 in the series and has often lamented his lack of productivity in both the NLCS and in all 10 games of the playoffs. Gary Carter was an exception in the Dodgers series. Over the five games, he batted .438 with a 7-for-16 run and had at least one hit in each of the five games. And Larry Parrish's performance was respectable with a 5-for-19 gig.

"I just didn't feel I contributed as much as I should have," Dawson said in the gloomy clubhouse. I haven't performed with authority in an entire month. I know I can't do everything, it requires a team effort: but we're not in the World Series."

"We didn't have enough hits," Expos shortstop Chris Speier lamented. It came down to the fifth game of a best-of-five series. You have to score more than one run."

"It's hard to believe there is no tomorrow," Carter sighed after the game. "It was one of the most exciting bad moments of my life. Every eye was on us. We were planning a team that at least for my generation had directed baseball and even became its symbol. The way it looks, the best team won. I've always wanted to get to the World Series, but a lot of greats aren't yet there."

Expos manager Jim Fanning chose to take some of the blame for the loss. "I feel so bad for Steve Rogers, but I gotta go with our best. I wish there was some way they could pin that loss to my name," Fanning said after the game. "We came so close. To stir up an entire country as we did was an unbelievable happening. Every one of these players should be proud of coming to within one out of making it to the World Series."

Can you blame Fanning for bringing in Rogers when the score was tied 1–1? It wasn't a totally urgent situation just then; but, on the other hand, it was a do-or-die game. The Game 5 winner would go to the World Series.

In my opinion, Fanning should have taken Rogers out after Ron Cey flied out deep to left to the warning track. He should have brought in southpaw Bill Lee or fellow lefty Woodie Fryman to face the lefty-swinging Monday.

In an interview with Don Rice of the Saskatoon *StarPhoenix* in 2012 at a 1981 Expos team reunion, Fanning chatted about his use of Rogers.

> He was the best pitcher in the National League in the last four or five weeks. I used to have those numbers in my head pretty much — he hardly gave up an earned run during that time. He pitched complete games regularly. Then he beat the Phillies twice in the playoffs. He beat the Dodgers. He was the best pitcher, maybe in Major League Baseball, at that time. Even if you go back farther, he was fantastic.
>
> He has taken some abuse for what happened. Admittedly, he says that he didn't have the sinker when he came in the game. It was my decision to do what I

did. He was the best pitcher in baseball. I know it was an unusual role except that the previous day when we were rained out on Sunday, he came to Galen Cisco, our pitching coach, and said, "Tomorrow's my day to throw. I can pitch tomorrow." And I said "That's good. You will not come in, in relief of a game in progress. You will come in to start an inning." So that's what happened.

Over the years, Fanning had always been gracious to me and many other writers when we would ask him about Blue Monday. Back in September of 2014, I asked him if he would talk to me for a flashback story I was writing about the 1979 and '80 Expos teams. He agreed, but with one stipulation. As an email from his wife, Marie, stated, "Jim insists no questions or conversation about what took place after December 31, 1980. Enough has been said and read about 1981." In another email, she wrote, "Lots of writers and so-called authors prefer to dwell on the loss. Shame on them."

Fanning had obviously grown weary of talking about Blue Monday.

I would have been one of those writers, but all I can say is that I'm grateful to Jim and Marie Fanning for allowing me access to them going back to 1988 when I arrived in Montreal. Along with Bob Elliott and Rich Griffin, I worked my way into Fanning's tight circle of respected journalists, and it meant a lot to me.

When I heard that Fanning had died on April 25, 2015, I broke down and cried. Then, as I was driving on Highway 401 near Toronto, I had to pull off to the side of the road to do a phone interview with a *Montreal Gazette* reporter about Jim. Again, I bawled. There has been only one other baseball figure whose death caused me to break down emotionally. That was San Diego Padres treasure Tony Gwynn, who had been so gracious and accommodating to me whenever I approached him at Olympic Stadium for interviews. He even surprised me in 2013 by returning my message seeking an interview for a book I co-authored with Bill Young on the 1994 Expos.

I knew Fanning had been ill with heart problems, a condition he had for an eternity. He even mentioned it to me, off the record, about 10 days before he died (I was interviewing him about Randy Johnson's starting out with the Expos). Out of respect for Fanning, I kept his heart issue under

Expos manager Jim Fanning was a coach at the 1982 All-Star Game held in Montreal.

wraps and didn't publicize it. But I didn't expect him to die so soon after we spoke. I had thought it was just a short-term issue. He was 87 when he died and had enjoyed a full life.

Marie Fanning also talked to me about her husband's lifelong battle with migraines, a condition that likely would have affected him in those stressful days attempting to clinch a playoff berth in New York, in the five-game series against the Phillies, and in the five-game series versus the Dodgers. When he stood in the dugout in Game 5 with his hands on his belt buckle and watched as Monday hit that home run, he must have been pretty stressed out.

"He had been having migraines since the age of six," Mrs. Fanning revealed. "His mom was also a migraine sufferer. Stress didn't help, but his migraines were an inherited condition. He took his migraines by the horns when they came; he knew how to handle them."

Chapter 29

Pitcher Had Fine Career

D ick Williams once called Steve Rogers a fraud.

Say what? Yes, he did. He did make this head-twisting point, decades ago, about the best pitcher in Expos franchise history. Imagine a manager talking that way about one of his own players in public. The declaration was pounced upon by the Montreal media.

You mean Williams dared talk that way about the winningest pitcher in the 36-season history of the Expos? The workhorse of the staff, who threw 129 complete games and hurled 37 shutouts?

"I think it's [widely] known that Dick didn't like pitchers because pitchers made him and other players mediocre ballplayers. Pitchers cut them down," Rogers told me. "I have heard [that] Dick and other managers didn't like pitchers. The vast majority of them made you feel that way. The vast majority didn't get along with pitchers. This is something I've learned more after the fact."

It's true, in some ways. Many successful managers didn't have much success as players. Williams's lifetime average was a solid .260, though; so, not bad at all.

Season	W	L	ERA	G	CG	IP
ROGERS'S GREAT MLB CAREER WITH EXPOS						
1973	10	5	1.54	17	7	134
1974	15	22	4.47	38	11	253.2
1975	11	12	3.29	35	12	251.2
1976	7	17	3.21	33	8	230
1977	17	16	3.10	40	17	301.2
1978	13	10	2.47	30	11	219
1979	13	12	3.00	37	13	248.2
1980	16	11	2.98	37	14	281
1981	12	8	3.42	22	7	160.2
1982	19	8	2.40	35	14	277
1983	17	12	3.23	36	13	273
1984	6	15	4.31	31	1	169.1
1985	2	4	5.68	8	1	38
	158	152	3.17	399	129	2,837.2

Source: Baseball Reference

Who would have ever believed that Rogers was a 60th-round pick? That's the crapshoot that is Major League Baseball's annual draft of amateur players.

The best pitcher in Expos history was drafted out of high school in 1967, somewhere between the 60th and the 67th rounds, but decided to go to university instead. An All-American in his senior year at the University of Tulsa, he went fourth overall in the secondary phase of the June 1971 MLB draft yet thought he shouldn't have to spend any time in the minor leagues. Cockiness, maybe? Or overconfidence?

"I went from being a 60th round pick to basically the first round," Rogers said. "My bonus would have been an apple. They didn't really know what to do with high-rounders out of college. I was the first guy in that

DICK WILLIAMS'S SON SPEAKS OUT

Dick Williams is speaking from the grave, so to speak. Through the words of his son Rick.

"Dad was not a fan of pitchers," the former Expos manager's son was saying, about the tumultuous relationship between his father and Expos ace Steve Rogers.

> He was not one to coddle pitchers. It wasn't one of his strong suits. He was not a fan of people and pitchers who made excuses or alibis and he didn't like pitchers who were weak to him or his teammates. That's a fact. I reiterate that. He wasn't cuddly with anybody.
>
> He had a number of quality pitching coaches. He did have tremendous relationships with pitchers who were in the form he wanted them to be. He liked guys like Jim Lonborg, Vida Blue, Catfish Hunter, Ken Holtzman, John Odom, Rollie Fingers, and Eric Show. He liked their intangibles: demeanour, gamesmanship, their approach, their hunger and fire. He loved giving the ball to Bill Lee and Ross Grimsley.
>
> And then there were other groups of pitchers where Steve Rogers falls in. That doesn't make Steve Rogers a bad person or a bad pitcher but he just might have fallen short of dad's expectations. Back then, Steve Rogers had a reputation as a clubhouse lawyer of some sort.

secondary phase that didn't go to the major leagues right off the bat. I really thought I got screwed over. I really thought I belonged in the majors."

Rogers soon found others thought otherwise, and he got a rude awakening in 1971 at the Triple-A level with the Winnipeg Whips of the International League. Especially in three trips to the mound to face the Rochester Red Wings, when he had his ass kicked.

"I was the red-headed stepchild," Rogers said, grinning. "It was like getting hit on the side of the head. It taught me I was not ready for the majors. I had to learn a little bit more."

Rogers went 3–10 with the Whips. Life in the minors that first season, his lack of success, and having to contend with Winnipeg's awful stadium sure opened up his eyes.

"Winnipeg had a bad Triple-A park right against the football field for the Winnipeg Blue Bombers," Rogers said. "The scoreboard was made of stark metal. It was all a nightmare. It was pretty dismal."

The Expos' Triple-A franchise moved to Virginia as the Peninsula Whips for 1972, and things got better at spring training, when pitching experts Larry Bearnarth and Cal McLish showed up to help him. Rogers gives them credit for shaping his career as a pitcher and it showed, even though his record was 2–6. The improvements started to take hold in 1973 when he went 7–6 in a combo season with Peninsula and Quebec City. (Rogers was relegated to Double-A with Quebec City but was promoted back to Triple-A.)

"Cal and Larry worked with me on developing the pitches I needed to get left-handed batters out. They gave me the ability to keep left-handed batters honest," Rogers said. "They taught me the cross-seam fastball. I always had the curveball and I had the slider."

By late in 1973, Rogers was in the majors for good, winning 10 and losing 5. In 1974, he went 15–22. He was one of the mainstays of the Expos' pennant race in only their fifth season of operation. Rogers would be solid in 1974 and 1975, but disaster hit the Expos in 1976 when they lost 107 games under Karl Kuehl.

"That was not fun," Rogers said of that season. "It was miserable losing 107 games."

As time went on, the Expos started to get a bit better, especially when Williams took over as manager. "The Expos felt that we had the talent level to win, and to win soon," Rogers said. "Nineteen seventy-seven was a very positive experience. We moved from Jarry Park to Olympic Stadium. You could pencil my name in for forty starts. Then, later on, I was a fraud. That bothered me, God rest Dick's soul. He had no problem with the way I pitched in 1977, and then after that, he never read it. In 1979 in Pittsburgh, we had won the first two games of the series and I'm sitting on

EXPOS WITH SENIORITY	
Player	**Seasons**
Steve Rogers	12¼
Tim Wallach	12¼
Gary Carter	11¼
Tim Raines	10½
Andre Dawson	10½
Bryn Smith	8¼
Larry Parrish	7¼
Warren Cromartie	7¼
Chris Speier	7¼
Woodie Fryman	7¼
Steve Renko	7¼
Vladimir Guerrero	7¼

Compiled by Danny Gallagher.

the bench and Dick tells the reporters, 'I'd love to go with a good pitcher like Charlie Lea or David Palmer, but I have to go with Rogers.'"

Insult for sure. Rogers then brought up his arm surgery September 12, 1978, when bone chips were removed by Dr. Frank Jobe in California.

"It wasn't Tommy John surgery," Rogers said. "Everybody wrote that it was minor elbow surgery, but I told the reporters at spring training in 1979 that it was not minor surgery. It was major surgery on my pitching elbow. It was one of those deals where they had to cut me open. It wasn't reconstructive surgery but I wanted to clear up something about what was written about my elbow.... Everybody was minimizing the fact that I had surgery."

Following the operation, Rogers called up Expos trainer Yvon Belanger, who had also worked for the NHL's Canadiens, and queried him on how he should undergo a rehabilitation program. Belanger wondered why Rogers's surgeon, Dr. Jobe, hadn't given him a program to follow. "I'll get back to you," Belanger told him.

Belanger never did. The training staff and the front office didn't put any plan in place, but pitching coach Jim Brewer suggested that Rogers be limited to 150 to 175 innings the following season (1979) and that the maximum number be stopped September 1. But Rogers was what he called "lights out" as August 1 rolled around. So he kept pitching and ended up throwing 248 innings. He said Williams didn't care if he went over the 175-inning allotment declared by Brewer.

In the end, the experiment of continuing to pitch backfired because his elbow began hurting late in the season and he couldn't help the Expos down the stretch drive. The Pirates won the NL East.

"I'd made the All-Star Game and I was regaining the ability to throw a baseball," Rogers said. "I did have some rough patches in late July. At one point, my arm gave out. I could tell you I had nothing. I had pitched my limit. One game I was pitching to Ray Knight of Cincinnati and I had him 0–2 and I wanted to throw a slider on the outside corner that he could chase. I threw the ball very poorly. I wasn't looking at home plate. He hit me with a line drive. I couldn't flinch with my right shoulder. My right arm went up against my body just below the elbow. I started to look at the arm. There was blood flow and trauma and the arm blew up the size of a softball. I got knocked out [of the game]. Luckily, it was all flesh, there was no serious damage. It was really depressing not being able to help. I left the team in the middle of a pennant race."

The decision to keep Rogers pitching would never have occurred in the current age where pitchers rarely throw complete games or are used cautiously if they are experiencing soreness.

"When I talk to people who don't know Steve Rogers," said fabled Expos announcer Dave Van Horne, "and I'm talking today's generation, I tell them, if you don't know who Steve Rogers is, then go to Baseball Reference, type in his name, and see his stats. Complete games, innings pitched. He was the total package." Van Horne continued,

> I remember interviewing Willie Stargell one time and he told me that Steve was the best right-handed pitcher he had ever faced, that he had the best slider of any right-handed pitcher he had ever faced. Back in 1974, Steve was close to losing 20 games and at one point, the media was asking manager Gene Mauch about that so Gene went to

Steve Rogers pitched for the Expos from 1973 to 1985.

Steve and said, "You're out there on a regular basis, not because of your losses, but because you are the best young pitcher we have." Rogers was that good. Gene was trying to take the pressure off Steve and put it on himself.

Without Steve Rogers, the Expos would never have gotten to the Dodgers series in 1981. In Game 5 vs. the Dodgers, Steve was healthy and he volunteered to pitch if he was needed. Jim Fanning said Steve was the best he had. He went head-to-head against Monday and Monday won the battle. On the first pitch from Steve, Monday just missed a home run so you knew Monday was on it.

If Rogers pitched today, he'd be a $20-million-a-year player. There are few pitchers around who could do what Rogers did.

"My all-time favourite Expo is Steve Rogers," said David Palmer, who was a teammate of Rogers for many seasons. "I told Steve he was the best right-hander I'd ever seen in baseball. His stuff was so good. He was just amazing. People don't understand that in 1979 he was coming off elbow surgery with no rehabilitation and still pitched close to 250 innings."

Said Rogers, "I can tell you they're over-protecting the pitchers today. Some pitchers are limited to 100 pitches per game. If they go over that, it's the manager's fault, the pitching coach's fault. The dynamics of the game have changed. My last contract, I signed a five-year deal. I don't remember the year, but Ruben Sierra won a salary-arbitration case in the 1990s and got $5 million. I'll never forget it. I was in the players association office and I told someone that Sierra in one year made more money than I did in my career."

Part Six

RICK MONDAY:
THE GUY WHO
HIT THAT HOMER

Chapter 30

Showing His Emotions

I t was a rare show of emotion by Rick Monday.

Realizing he had smashed a dramatic home run to put the Dodgers ahead of the Expos in the top of the ninth inning in the deciding game of the NLCS, after he rounded first base, he punched his left hand up into the air in triumph. As he rounded second, he did it again, though not quite as hard. He almost slipped and fell going toward third.

After looking at that YouTube video a number of times, I thought I would ask Monday if there had been any other moment in his baseball career when he got so emotional.

"Off the top of my head, one other time," he told me.

We then got sidetracked into talking about something else. Monday wasn't going to expand on the original thought until I followed up, so I asked, "So what happened the other time?"

So Monday confessed that it's the first time he's told this story to a reporter, and he's telling me somewhat reluctantly. It was something he hadn't even disclosed in his 2006 book *Rick Monday's Tales from the Dodgers Dugout*.

"That would have been my rookie year in Kansas City," he began. "But it all goes back to Los Angeles years earlier."

He was just a kid then, maybe 12 or 13. He had made the trek to the famed Los Angeles Coliseum, about 30 miles from his home in Santa Monica. Monday doesn't know the exact year, but it would have been no earlier than 1958, the Dodgers' first season in L.A.

"It's a Sunday afternoon game between the Dodgers and Cubs. I'm sitting down the left-field line, six rows back," Monday related. "Ernie Banks hits a ball and it lands a couple of rows behind me. It ricochets and I catch the ball. After the game, I knew the Dodgers' team bus was inside this fence. I recognized this Dodgers player. I politely told him that I had caught this ball from Ernie Banks and I asked him, 'Could you please sign my ball?' Very silently and very politely, the player took me off to the side and said, 'I'm really in a big hurry.'"

He didn't sign the ball, and it was something that Monday never forgot. He was very disappointed and heartbroken that this highly recognized Los Angeles player wouldn't sign his ball. The guy couldn't take three or four seconds out of his time before getting on the bus to give a kid an autograph? Hrmmph.

So years later, the plot continued, the tale kept on winding. Monday had become a member of the major-league ranks. Monday would have been 21 years old at this point, so it was close to 10 years since he had been turned down by the player.

"What goes around comes around," Monday said. "I got a little bit older, a bit bigger, and a lot better. I was playing for Kansas City in 1967 and we were playing Detroit. The Tigers were trying to win the pennant."

Monday is uncertain of the exact date, so I click on retrosheet.org and go to 1967, check out Kansas City game logs, and discover that the date he's referring to is June 17. It's the seventh inning at Tiger Stadium, and the guy who turned Monday down years earlier was pitching for the Tigers after years as a star with the Dodgers.

"So I'm facing this same player who very gently and very politely took me off to the side ... and said he was in a big hurry," Monday said. "So I get a base hit off this pitcher. I started to run up and down, yelling at him, 'Thanks for not signing my ball. Thanks for not signing my ball.' I kept repeating it. 'Thanks for not signing my ball.'"

The Tigers pitcher looked over at Monday and must have thought there was something wrong with him. The pitcher, of course, would not have remembered the young man who had asked him for an autograph. But Monday sure remembered him.

Years went by without Monday getting another chance to talk to the pitcher. That is, until one day in the late 1980s or early '90s when the two men attended a Dodgers fantasy camp in Vero Beach, Florida.

"I see this pitcher. Not only do I see him, he's at the next table," Monday said as the suspense mounted. "So I told him I was glad to tell him this story. I told him he didn't sign my ball. He turned out to be one of the nicest people you'd ever want to meet. One of the nicest people I ever met. He said that when I was yelling at him [on the field], he thought I was nuts."

The pitcher's name? Johnny Podres. He was a fabulous pitcher for the Dodgers in the 1950s and 1960s. He was 146–101 for the Dodgers, beginning in Brooklyn and ending in Los Angeles before he wound down his career with the Tigers. He pitched a 2–0 shutout in Game 7 of the 1955 World Series to give the Dodgers their only World Series championship in Brooklyn.

Podres would go on to be a pitching coach for an amazing 23 seasons in the majors between 1973 and 1996 for the San Diego Padres, Boston Red Sox, Minnesota Twins, and Philadelphia Phillies. Podres died in 2008, two years after Monday's book came out. Monday was not ready to rock the pitcher's boat while he was still alive — so he waited until now to tell this story.

Chapter 31

The Wrath of the Fans

Over the years, Rick Monday has felt the wrath of many Montrealers and other Canadians — he's been approached in public washrooms, while going through customs and immigration, while dining in restaurants, and most recently on social media.

One day in 1982, the year following his epic home run, while he tended to business in a lavatory not far from the Olympic Stadium press box, an Expos fan stepped in to the urinal next to him and blurted out, "You ruined our franchise."

That same year, Monday and teammate Steve Yeager dropped into the famous Sir Winston Churchill Pub on Crescent Street in Montreal for a bite to eat. Monday and Yeager ordered drinks and were looking at the menu when the manager came over.

"We're going to have to ask you to leave," he told them.

"But it's only seven, and the kitchen is closed at ten," Monday retorted.

"Yes, but there are six guys at the other table who want a piece of you. We don't want to see any fights."

So Monday and Yeager got up and left.

Much later, in the final year of the Expos' operation in 2004, Monday and his wife Barbaralee were visiting Old Montreal and thought for a moment they were running into more fan opposition.

"We found a lovely little restaurant on a cobblestone street," Monday recalled. "They spoke practically no English. We walk into the restaurant and it's about 50 feet to the reception area. Then there's this host coming to see me. I thought they were going to tell us we couldn't come in because of the home run. So the host says, 'You can't come in! You can't come in!' But it ends up we couldn't come in because there was a kitchen fire. It was comical."

Sandwiched between those adventures was the time Monday checked in at immigration at Montreal's Dorval Airport one day, only to be delayed. "It was the secondary phase of immigration and they put me in the back room to cool my heels," Monday said. "The gentleman was looking at the computer and he smiled. And I said, 'Does this have anything to do with the home run?'"

Expos executive assistant Marcia Schnaar recalled that sometime in the 1980s she ran across Monday as he walked toward the Expos' spring-training offices in West Palm Beach. "And the poor gentleman, before I said anything, said, 'Please don't say anything!' I guess, by the time he reached my office, everyone he met must have said something to him.

"I did talk with Rick Monday, just not about the home run," she added, smiling.

Everyone remembers where they were that day in October of 1981. It was hip to be an Expos fan. The team had captured the hearts and imagination of baseball fans in Canada from coast to coast. The Blue Jays had been in existence for five years, but their following nation-wide was miniscule compared to the Expos'.

"Whenever I see that home run, I still cringe and probably always will," said Expos fan Dave Bustin of Dartmouth, Nova Scotia.

> Don't mention Monday's name. I know we will see or hear Monday's name forever. It's just that when I hear or see the name, that home run is the only thing I can think of. I've never met Monday. He may be a great guy, I don't know. He had a long major-league career and accomplished things other than that home run.... I was lying on my living room floor watching the game in Dartmouth. I

was 10. I had just started getting into baseball. I was very disappointed when the Expos couldn't have at least tied it up in the bottom of the ninth.

In Montreal, E.J. Hansen related his story:

I was 15 years old … a student at Bishop Whelan High School in Lachine, Quebec. I had bought four tickets for each of the home games in the Phillies and Dodgers series. I was there for the Friday night game and the Saturday afternoon game of the Los Angeles series with friends and my cousin. On Sunday, my cousin and I had gone and the game was called off. I had school on the Monday and walked out at 10:30 in the morning to get on the 191 bus by myself and headed to the Big O. I met my dad, who was there with some buddies and I sat with them in the 200 section under the overhang behind home plate. My mom was upset I missed school. I had to get my dad to write me a fake dentist's note. I can remember it like it was yesterday. My dad passed a few years ago. When I think of him now, I think of that day. I don't cry much, but I did that day.

It's weird, as the conventional wisdom was that Bill Lee would have been a better option than Steve Rogers to pitch to Monday, but Rogers had been so good that month that it wasn't a move that you could really fault. It's done so much now with guys like Jon Lester, Madison Bumgarner, and Andrew Miller, but it wasn't so commonplace then [to use a starting pitcher in relief] and I don't think Rogers had done it much before. I guess a lefty/lefty matchup should have been thought of. I always wondered what Dick Williams would have done. The ball Ron Cey hit should've clued Rogers in to the fact that maybe he didn't have his good stuff that day.

Steve Rogers blows a kiss at a ball at ExposFest in Montreal, March 25, 2018.

In Moncton, New Brunswick, Gail Johnson recalls vividly that day in the fall of 1981:

> That day was the beginning of my lifelong love-hate relationship with baseball. Mostly love, though. I was an Expos fan. I was nine years old at the time. I had just started watching baseball that summer with my father, who was a lifelong Dodgers fan. When the Expos lost that day, dad was so happy and I started crying and ran to my bedroom. I remember seeing Jim Fanning's face and feeling so bad for him. It was the first time of many that baseball made

me cry over the years. Dad feels bad to this day that he was so happy and his little nine-year-old baseball fan was in tears. I became a Dodgers fan after following Tim Wallach's coaching career in that great organization. Wallach has left the Dodgers, but I'm a Dodgers fan for life now. Every year on Blue Monday I wonder what might have been. Many years later, in 2016, I saw the Dodgers clinch the pennant in person … at Dodger Stadium, which was a dream come true. And I almost forgive them for Blue Monday.

Adding a Canadian Prairie voice was Doug Fast of Saskatoon:

Blue Monday is such an open wound. It was such a letdown. That was our shot and it sucked. I can't understand why Fanning would put Steve Rogers in instead of Jeff Reardon. I loved Jeff Reardon. He had that swagger. I liked the finish on his delivery. The way he was throwing so hard, it was almost like he was out of control. Rogers was in control with his delivery, but Reardon, he reared back. He was a bad-ass guy.

And there's Montreal blogger Mark Deutsch, who was 16 in 1981. His tale is remarkable in that he tuned in for every darn second of the game on television. He refrained from going to the loo for fear he would miss something. As he says in his blog,

I watched every single moment of it right down to the heartbreaking end. Every second. Every play. I didn't even go to the bathroom. While I always scored the game, which meant recording every detail of the game on a scoresheet, something I had done for about every Expos' game for as long as I was able, I did not score this game. I sat in my bedroom on my bed watching.… Jim Fanning was a very nice man and a decent general manager, but as a manager, he was neither qualified nor prepared.

208

I remember turning to a fellow reporter in the press box at the Big O and muttering something like, "He didn't just do that did he?" Steve Garvey, Ron Cey, Pedro Guerrero, or someone like that, but Rick fucking Monday? I remember heading down to the clubhouses, still stunned by the Expos coming this close to the World Series, and I could hear the Dodgers singing the Expos' rally song, "The Happy Wanderer" — "Val-deri, val-dera!" — from the hallway as their cookie-cutter Hollywood wives shared champagne outside the room. I also recall spotting NBC's Bryant Gumbel, that arrogant pompous ass, wearing fur gloves that reached up to his elbows, showing North America just how cold it was up here in chilly Montreal, with a smirk on his face.

— Broadcaster John Gallagher, who attended the Blue Monday game

But the best fan memory or best fan quote about October 19, 1981, came from Greg Leonard, a Montrealer currently living in Philadelphia. Without blinking an eyelash, he told me, "Forget about American Pie. Blue Monday was the day the music died for us in Montreal. It's a visceral sentiment."

This brings us to Roland Hemond, one of Fanning's friends and a long-time big-league executive. He was 52 at the time and showed up for Game 5 in his capacity as Chicago White Sox general manager. Hemond isn't out to badmouth Monday, but was feeling a little sad for Fanning. He was one of many executives from other teams in attendance. Jackie Robinson's widow Rachel was also there in the stands with the Dodgers entourage.

"I was actually at the game that day and rooting for Les Expos, hoping they would win the World Series, since my mother is of French-Canadian ancestry," Hemond recalled. "I was also pulling for Jim Fanning, since he had managed in the Milwaukee Braves' system when I was assistant to John Mullen, the farm and scouting director."

I asked Monday himself if it bothered him that so many fans loathe him. "No, not at all. That doesn't bother me," Monday replied. "What does bother me is those people who have negative thoughts about Steve Rogers and want to criticize [him]. This guy had a tremendous career. I marvelled at his competiveness on the field. He did not let up one pitch; he did not let up on one hitter. What gets lost, unfortunately, is the tremendous career Steve had. He's been nothing but a gentleman before, during, and after the event. It was just two guys who happened to compete. He wasn't bragging that I hit less than .200 against him. I had a tremendous amount of respect for him then and I have even more respect for him now."

Chapter 32

Cutting Ties

When Robert James (Rick) Monday beat the Expos with that dramatic home run in October 1981, his father wasn't at the game.

When Rick Monday Jr. was on the cusp of turning 10, one of the most distressing things in his life occurred. His father by the same given name just up and left, leaving his son in a broken home.

At age 44, in 1955, Robert James Monday Sr. decided he didn't want to be married to his wife Nelda anymore, after 14 years of matrimony, and he abandoned his son in the process.

"Everybody deals with something, and you deal with it," Monday Jr. said in 2017. "My father decided to pack up and leave when I was 10 years old. He wanted to live somewhere else. I didn't see him for years. Then one day, I heard a voice above the dugout. I had not seen or heard from him in at least eight or nine years."

Monday recalled that he "just said hello" to his estranged father in the stands but that was it. There was no conversation, just resentment on the son's part. The brief exchange took place at a time when the father realized his son had blossomed into a decent baseball player and wanted to make contact again to see if they could reconcile. The son would have nothing to do with reconciliation. It was around the time Monday began playing major-league ball with the Kansas City Athletics.

"I moved on," he said. "Here's the deal: Not to put the blame on him, I moved on. You survive. I had a mother. I was fortunate to have a mother who was the salt of the earth, one of the greatest ladies. In my eyes, one of the greatest people I've ever been around. She did a magnificent job as a single parent."

Did Monday ever try to connect again with his father later in life?

"No, I moved on," he said.

Rick Monday Sr. and Nelda grew up in Batesville, Arkansas, and were married there on July 7, 1941, according to online reports. Four and a half years later, on November 20, Rick Jr. was born. In October 1946, the Monday clan decided to head west and settled in Santa Monica, California.

"I have no recollection of Batesville," Rick Jr. said.

Little is known of what the father did after he left the marriage. But as I sat down at a library in West Palm Beach, Florida, to look at *Palm Beach Post* microfilm in the spring of 2017, I noticed that Monday Sr. died in Palm Beach on October 6, 1998, at age 81. Nelda died a few days after 9/11, also at age 81; ironically, she died on the date she was born in 1920 in Floyd, Arkansas.

Chapter 33

Beanball

Rick Monday's career never panned out the way it was projected. He never quite lived up to his press clippings. He wasn't a superstar. He wasn't a star. Yet, he did enjoy a solid major-league career that lasted 19 seasons.

He's the answer to one of the biggest trivia questions in major-league baseball history: who was the very first pick in the very first major-league draft of amateur free-agent players in 1965?

How did it feel to be the Number-1 pick? Monday more or less deflected the question. "Nobody knew. It never happened before. We didn't know the system would work," he told me, 52 years after he, a star player at Arizona State University, had been selected by Charlie Finley's Kansas City Athletics.

The novelty of staging a free-agent draft of amateur high-school, college, and sandlot players on June 9, 1965, was something major-league owners and commissioner Bowie Kuhn had been mulling over for years. Prior to this, amateur players anywhere could be signed by any major-league team.

"This I can say, every year I smile at every first pick," Monday told me. "They know what the expectations are. If he's a hitter and gets two hits,

FIRST ROUND OF FIRST MAJOR-LEAGUE DRAFT IN JUNE 1965

Player	Team	Pos.	School Drafted From
Rick Monday	Kansas City Athletics	OF	Arizona State University, Tempe
Les Rohr	New York Mets	LHP	Billings West HS, Billings, Mont.
Joe Coleman	Washington Senators	RHP	Natick HS, Natick, Mass.
Alex Barrett	Houston Astros	SS	Atwater HS, Atwater, Calif.
Billy Conigliaro	Boston Red Sox	OF	Swampscott HS, Swampscott, Mass.
Rick James	Chicago Cubs	SS	Coffee HS, Florence, Ala.
Ray Fosse	Cleveland Indians	C	Marian HS, Marian, Ill.
John Wyatt	Los Angeles Dodgers	SS	Bakersfield HS, Bakersfield, Calif.
Eddie Leon	Minnesota Twins	SS	University of Arizona, Tucson
Doug Dickerson	Pittsburgh Pirates	OF	Ensley HS, Birmingham, Ala.
Jim Spencer	California Angels	1B	Andover HS, Glen Birnie, Md.
Dick Grant	Milwaukee Braves	1B	Watertown HS, Watertown, Mass.
Gene Lamont	Detroit Tigers	P	Hiwatha HS, Kirkland, Ill.
Al Gallagher	San Francisco Giants	1B	Santa Clara HS, Santa Clara, Calif.
Scott McDonald	Baltimore Orioles	RHP	Marquette HS, Yakima, Wash.
Bernie Carbo	Cincinnati Reds	3B	Livonia HS, Franklin, Mich.
Ken Plesha	Chicago White Sox	C	Notre Dame U, Notre Dame, Ind.
Mike Adamson	Philadelphia Phillies	RHP	Point Loma HS, San Diego
Bill Burbach	New York Yankees	RHP	Wahlert HS, Dickeyville, Wis.
Joe DiFabio	St. Louis Cardinals	RHP	Delta State U, Cleveland, Miss.

people will say why not four hits? If a pitcher strikes out four, why not 10? For the first pick every year, the expectations are very, very high."

Was there a lot of pressure being the first pick? I asked Monday this, not wanting to get too inquisitive or to imply that he was disappointed in his career.

"Pressure? Pressure is from within, that you can't let anyone down," he said. "The journey is just beginning. Getting to Major League Baseball is difficult. Staying for an extended period of time is that much more difficult. I had some injuries during my career. I got hit in the face by a pitch that affected my eyesight. I got hit by Gary Peters of the White Sox at Comiskey Park."

Monday was in his first season with the Kansas City Athletics and Retrosheet research shows that lefty Peters hit Monday with that pitch on June 3, 1967. The pitch caught Monday on the right side of the face during the first inning of the game and he was taken to hospital. Peters would later say that he was only protecting his teammates, especially Canadian-born Canadian Baseball Hall of Fame member Pete Ward, who had somehow raised the ire of Kansas City pitchers earlier that season and was plunked a number of times. As Monday recalls,

> It was a little unsettling to wake up in an ambulance. I got hit … just under the cheekbone, just near the nose. It was similar to what happened to Tony Conigliaro. It's not all rosy. I had to have Achilles tendon surgery in 1979. Bobby Tolan had it, too. You have to have a certain degree of toughness. It's not all fun and games at the ballpark. You can get frustrated. You have to be physically, mentally, and internally tough and very dedicated.
>
> Look at it this way; you look at the brass ring. When we were young at Los Angeles Coliseum, there was the magical green carpet. I was mesmerized to have the opportunity to play. My Uncle Jim had played some good amateur ball and I was playing Pony League for players 13 or 14 [years old]. A coach came up to me and said, "How would you like to play pro baseball?" I said I would love to. The coach said, "You're 14, you have a chance." That was reinforcement for me. Coach Ruben Navarro filled a void.

After a few years, Monday would venture up to Fairbanks, Alaska, from California to continue his baseball education with the Alaska Goldpanners before heading to Arizona State. His Fairbanks teammates included future major-leaguers Graig Nettles, Jimy Williams, Gary Sutherland, and, oh, this pitcher by the name of Tom Seaver.

"It was a great league up there," Monday said. "It was an absolutely great adventure for three months. As a job on the side, Graig Nettles and I were part of a construction crew. We were loading and unloading tractor trailers. As we were loading into an 18-wheeler truck one day, someone came along and said, 'We can't have you doing that because we could be sued.' Then they put us on construction yard work, and then one day it was raining like you wouldn't believe, big, big drops and hard. They said the weather wasn't conducive to work and actually we were fired from the job. I ended up helping out the grounds crew and I worked at a car dealership selling cars. I sold a car in the first hour."

By the following year, Monday was taking in the sights and sounds of Arizona State, but not before Dodgers scout Tommy Lasorda had tried to sign him on the spot for the Dodgers.

"I had a Dodgers uniform in my closet at home," Monday recalled.

Monday would have preferred to sign with the Dodgers, but his mother Nelda put her fist down, insisting that he go to university and get some education. Lasorda kept upping his offer, finally stopping at $20,000. That's where ASU baseball coach Bobby Winkles entered the picture to tell Nelda and her son that he would take care of him.

If there were three people who helped make Arizona State University's men's baseball team what it is today, they would be Winkles, Monday, and Reggie Jackson, the same Jackson the Expos tried to sign in the fall of 1976.

After playing in the Chicago White Sox minor-league system for most of the 1950s, Winkles was hired to be the first-ever coach of ASU's varsity baseball team late in 1958.

Though the early years at ASU were lean for Winkles, his patience paid off in 1963 when a standout player arrived: Rick Monday.

"Rick was going to get a lot of money from the Dodgers, but his mother said he was going to college," Winkles told me. "A scout told me to get over there to see Rick and his mother. They had a little two-room place. I sat down in the kitchen and we started talking. I asked her where she was from."

Turned out they were both from Arkansas, Nelda from Batesville and Winkles from Tuckerman and later Swifton, just 45 minutes from Batesville.

With that, Mrs. Monday quickly said, "Where do we sign?"

Funny thing, as Winkles said, "Rick wasn't very happy" signing the contract to go to Arizona State. This was 1963.

As a freshman in 1964, Monday wasn't permitted under NCAA rules to play on the varsity team. By 1965, Monday was on the varsity team as a sophomore and he helped Winkles and the Sun Devils to the national championship and the College World Series. During regular-season play, Monday batted .385 with 34 extra-base hits. He remembered:

> We were 54–8 that season, including the post-season. Bobby Winkles did a good job of protecting us before the draft. When the draft came up, there was no cable network. It was not on the MLB Network. There was no internet, no Twitter, no cellphones. We were in uniform in right field. Winkles wanted us to stay focused on baseball. He was saying that when the draft takes place, when the media comes, that we stay together as a group. I'm very glad that he told us that. Coach Winkles kept the media away. One reporter did ask [me] prior to the draft, "You will be the Number-1 pick. What do you think?"

Charlie Finley showed up to see Monday in Omaha, Nebraska, the start of a short relationship that went sour. Monday didn't go into a lot of detail, but I could tell he was simmering a bit about the way Finley dealt with him:

> After the game, considering Kansas City was the worst team, attorneys came to me and told me what baseball was doing. They said we could challenge the draft. They wanted to see if I wouldn't sign and take the case to court. I was told it might take two or three years in court and I said I was not interested.

Rick Monday in ASU
uniform in 1965.

That set the stage for contract negotiations between Monday and
Finley. Monday's mother Nelda got involved in the talks, as did Monday's
Uncle Bob.

> The contract did not happen immediately. My uncle
> threw a ringer into it. Finley wanted to talk about dollars;
> we countered with tax-free dollars. It was reported that I
> signed for $104,000, but it was much more than that. We
> discussed other things that took place with Finley. I was
> close to filing a lawsuit against him about certain things.

Monday stopped there. He wouldn't reveal exactly what Finley did to
raise the ire in him. In the end, playing in the majors was more important

than challenging Finley and baseball in court. "I was taking [what] I felt was the best chance in the most rapid fashion with Kansas City," Monday said.

"Rick Monday was a very unusual kid, such a regular person," Winkles said. "He was such a quiet guy. If you said 'jump' to Rick, he'd say, 'How high, coach?' He was that kind of guy…. Monday was always such a good player, I mean a really good player."

The way Duffy Dyer talked, Monday was a superstar in the making. Dyer was one of Monday's teammates at Arizona State. "Monday, in fact, was very good. We thought he would be the Hall of Famer more than Reggie," Dyer said. "Rick was already a very good centre-fielder, very good defensively. He could hustle and run above average, a very good hitter in college. We thought he would be a very, very good major-leaguer. Funny thing, Reggie came along and played centre field. At the time, I thought Rick would be the better player. He was polished, a good base runner. Reggie was not quite as polished as Rick. Reggie was not as good as Rick defensively. He was a good thrower but he wasn't very accurate."

Entering into the fray of discussion about Monday was another former ASU teammate, Jack Smitheran.

"Oh, God, what a good guy. Rick was just a great talent, but never acted that way," Smitheran said. "I always appreciated the way he conducted himself. He came as a freshman and there would be times the freshmen would play against the varsity team. I'll never forget that there were times when he would go out three or four times in a game and he'd come into the clubhouse with a big smile. He'd say, 'I didn't do that good today but there's always tomorrow.' He put things in the right perspective, that there was another day."

As for that comparison with Jackson, Smitheran said, "Rick was more polished than Reggie, much, much more refined than Reggie. Rick was way ahead of Reggie as far as defending and knowledge. I remember Rick running. He could really run. He was hustling all the time down to first base. He had special talents. He was a consummate teammate. That's Rick. I respected him more than anything. He made an impact."

Monday commenced his professional career in the Single-A Northwest loop with the Broncos in Lewiston, Idaho. Following the season, Monday and his Lewiston teammate and future pitching-coach icon Dave Duncan travelled to San Diego for boot camp with the U.S. Marine Corps.

Rick Monday throws out the first pitch at an Arizona State University Sun Devils game. Looking on, from left to right, are Tony Alesci, Ralph Vasquez, Skip Hancock, Jim Merrick, Sal Bando, Ralph Carpenter, and John Pavlik. All but Vasquez were Monday's teammates.

Rick Monday in his days
playing for Oakland.

Monday played most of the 1966 season in Double-A in Mobile, Alabama, before getting called up to the majors by Kansas City in September.

"Rick was a very talented guy, which made him the first pick in the first-ever draft," said Sal Bando, a teammate of his at Arizona State and later with the Oakland Athletics. "He had power, he could run, throw, there wasn't anything he couldn't do. He played hard, he came to win. If he didn't have a good game here and there, it didn't bother him. Reggie had more power, he was a little stronger. Rick had the speed. They were two different types of players. Rick was a very polished defensive player. Reggie played football and it took him a while to get a groove in baseball. So much was expected of him."

In the end, it was Jackson who made it into the Hall of Fame, not Monday. Yet, Monday forged a solid major-league career of his own over more than 19 seasons. When I told Monday that Dyer had said he felt

Monday was destined for Cooperstown, not Jackson, he again deflected his answer. "Reggie came after me," Monday said, without making any direct comment about Dyer's prediction.

The kicker in the conversations about Monday versus Jackson came from Bobby Winkles. Something about intensity. "Reggie was more intense I would think than Rick. For whatever reason, for some reason, I don't know why, Rick didn't get a good shot at being a Number-1 player. He was just a quiet guy. There were times when Reggie would show up at baseball batting practice with his football pads on in the batting cage. There was a lot of talk that Reggie didn't do this and didn't do that but he caused me no trouble. He would run out every ball harder than anyone I have seen."

Chapter 34

Rescuing the U.S. Flag

Rick Monday, then playing for the Chicago Cubs, had been patrolling centre field when it all happened: April 25, 1976.

Out of left field came two people holding an American flag. They plopped it down on the grass at Dodger Stadium, soaked it in lighter fluid, and were about to burn it when the quick-thinking Monday swooped in, grabbed the flag, and kept going before they could get the fire to catch.

The two culprits watched him go, in utter astonishment: William Errol Thomas, or William Errol Morris, and his son, 11, who was never identified because of his age.

Some reports say the father, who was born in Eldon, Missouri, threw the lighter fluid at Monday, but by then the Cubs player was far out of range. Monday handed the flag off to Dodgers pitcher Doug Rau while Dodgers manager Tommy Lasorda raged profanities at the protestors.

This being America's bicentennial year, the protestors had apparently been lamenting the poor treatment of Native American Indians. After the game Monday asked for the flag but was told it was being kept for the police investigation. The next day, the Illinois State Legislature voted May 4 as Rick Monday Day. A month later, with the Dodgers in town to play

Rick Monday rescues American flag from protestors, April 25, 1976.

the Cubs at Wrigley Field, Dodgers GM Al Campanis presented the flag to Monday. He has kept it ever since.

Monday had more than a passing interest in saving the flag, not just because he was a proud American, but because he had served in the U.S. Marines as a reserve, beginning in the 1960s.

"That was the wrong thing to do," Monday said about the protestors. "I had served in the Marines. I requested if I could have that flag when the case was over. The Dodgers got in touch with me. I was given a cassette recording of that day in 1984, after I had stopped playing.

"[In 1984] I was at a meeting in Universal City at a cable television station because I was looking to get into the sports broadcasting business. The Dodgers cable TV people [had] recognized the person in the tape. The man said he saw the video of me with the flag. Someone had shot it on his own camera. No one knew it existed. It was a 16 mm bumped over to video tape. The only thing besides the cassette was a photograph that got James Roark a Pultizer Prize nomination."

Roark was a photographer with the Los Angeles tabloid *Herald Examiner* and had been stationed in the photo pit on the first-base side at Dodger Stadium when he noticed the commotion in centre field. With a Nikon F2S camera sporting a 300 mm 4.5 lens, he snapped and snapped. He drove back to the paper's downtown office and told his boss that he had a good photo to run the next day.

Sure enough, when the negatives came back from the darkroom, Roark had a winner. It was possibly the best photograph he had ever taken. Years later, after Monday had joined the Dodgers, he met up with Roark, who presented Monday with a print of the momentous shot. Roark had titled the photo "A Run for Old Glory."

When the Hearst Corporation decided to shutter the newspaper, Roark found himself out of a job. The company donated the paper's archives to the Los Angeles Public Library, which to this day holds the rights to the photos: the photo in this book was obtained from the LAPL. Roark went on to do some freelance photo work but was eventually reduced to working as a cook in Portland, Oregon. On October 15, 1995, after finishing a shift at Richard's restaurant in Portland, Roark was mugged and killed by four people during a robbery.

"The irony of the flag is that it has been very active," Monday told me. "It was never intended to be destroyed. My wife Barbaralee and I have moved it around the country to raise money for military charities."

The battered Stars and Stripes banner that Monday keeps at home in Vero Beach, Florida, is so popular that even the Baseball Hall of Fame in Cooperstown, New York, wants to get its hands on it. But it's always been Monday's policy that he will not give it up, sell it, or loan it to anyone. He has had offers of $1 million for it and turned them down. After playing some 19 seasons in the majors with a sizeable pension from the players association, and the fact that he remains on the Dodgers' payroll as an announcer, Monday has no need of any extra income.

"The Hall of Fame requested the flag," Monday said. "My stance is that it has been in a storage area behind a piece of glass. It's in our hands, in our control. It was more than just a flag. I think not so much about what I did that day in 1976 but the reaction of people. I still get letters from people not so much about the incident but about the flag representing the rights

225

and the freedoms of the people who have served their country, some of whom have paid the ultimate price. That's what makes me proud. Oddly enough, my wife has gone on the internet and we have heard from five or six people who were in the background of the photo. Not long ago, I ran into a couple who had been at the game."

Rick and Barbaralee, and sometimes just Barbaralee alone, travel across the country to show the flag at charity events. In 2008, the Mondays met for dinner at the White House with then president George H.W. Bush and his wife. It was a chance to show the Bush duo the flag.

"Whenever we can, we stop at every veterans hospital," Monday said. "We've been to the medical centre in DC and the White House. The flag is still active in our country. It was not a brand new flag. It smelled of lighter fluid. One time, it went across 14 states in 14 days to Dodger Stadium. It crossed the desert when it was 120 degrees and you could actually smell the lighter fluid. The flag has been all across the country. It has helped a lot of people."

As legendary *Los Angeles Times* baseball columnist Ross Newhan looked back to compare Monday's home run off of Rogers and the flag rescue, he ventured to say that most people in Los Angeles probably don't remember Monday for the home run.

Rick Monday displays the flag he rescued, with ASU baseball coach Tracy Smith.

"I would be willing to bet that if you asked Los Angeles fans what they would recall about Rick Monday, they'd say catching the flag, because the generations change. I think younger fans might not even be aware of the home run," Newhan said.

"With him rescuing the flag from being burned, he'll be known for that for the rest of his life," said 1981 Dodgers pitching coach Ron Perranoski.

Monday's home run would rank just south in importance in Dodgers history behind badly injured Kirk Gibson's pinch-hit blast off of Dennis Eckersley in Game 1 of the 1988 World Series. As Newhan put it,

> I talked to several of the Dodgers' players — Rick Monday, Mike Scioscia — and they were on the same point that as dramatic as Monday's home run was to win the series, that they didn't have time to savour it. They went right into the World Series. That was that. Because the World Series was right on top of that, I hate to say it, but it lost a bit of its glamour. Perhaps, it got lost in the glow of the World Series.
>
> Certainly, no question, the Gibson home run is the most dramatic in Los Angeles Dodgers history and Monday's is a close second, I would think. Mike Scioscia's home run off of Dwight Gooden in the 1989 ALCS was pretty dramatic because Gooden was so overpowering. Chuck Essegian's two pinch-hit home runs in the 1959 World Series against the White Sox were also big moments in Dodgers history.

Curious about the ill feeling that appears to exist between Monday and Gibson, I asked Monday if he had ever talked with or shared stories with Gibson about their iconic home runs.

"I never talked to him about anything," Monday said, succinctly.

I didn't press the issue. Whether Monday is envious of the attention Gibson has received for his home run, I don't know; but, clearly, Monday doesn't like Gibson much.

"Gibson is a laconic guy," Newhan said. "I got along with him fine. A lot of writers didn't. He was not a malcontent. His one goal was to perform on the field and win. He wouldn't let anything get in the way of that."

Chapter 35

"We Are the Champions"

The 1981 World Series was barely over before Rick Monday was invited to be in a quartet to belt out the Queen song "We Are the Champions." And Monday and Dodgers teammates Steve Yeager, Jay Johnstone, and Jerry Reuss certainly didn't know that they would soon be performing it on *The Tonight Show Starring Johnny Carson.*

"I had worked on ABC television the previous five seasons," Monday said in 2017, as he laid out the background leading up to the gig with Carson. "I had gotten a call about doing a precursor to *Saturday Night Live* called *Friday.* It was a day or two after the World Series ended. What the people had in mind was that we would do it for charity. Any or all monies would go to a children's charity, so we were all in. So the thought was that we would come and do a cameo appearance or sketch on the ABC network show *Friday.*"

Next thing he knew, Monday was in the ABC parking lot on a pay-phone singing "Do-Re-Mi" as a bit of an audition. The audition was a success. Monday, Yeager, Reuss, and Johnstone got together because they were fairly close — Yeager was Monday's roommate on road trips and Johnstone was born on the same day in the same year as Monday (November 20, 1945).

A promotional sleeve for the Dodgers' song.

"So pretty soon we were going into the studio to record one afternoon … we did vocals the very next night," Monday said. "We did a rehearsal at a talent stage. Tony Orlando choreographed something we were doing for two hours."

Monday and his mates — officially recognized as the Big Blue Wrecking Crew — got a call, and on just 12 hours' notice, the producers of NBC's *The Tonight Show* wanted the quartet to come on and show off their pipes.

"On *The Tonight Show*, you don't go on recorded," Monday said. "It was always live, so we had to rehearse."

To get on with Carson was almost unheard of. There were lineups of people and entertainers wanting to get on the show. PR types were continually

WHERE ARE THE 1981 DODGERS NOW?*

Player	Where he resides	What he's up to
Dusty Baker	Granite Bay, Calif.	Special advisor to Giants' CEO
Mark Bradley	Elizabethtown, Ken.	Unknown
Ron Cey	Los Angeles	Dodgers ambassador
Joe Ferguson	San Francisco	Retired
Terry Forster	Santee, Calif.	Retired
Pepe Frias	Dominican Republic	Retired
Steve Garvey	Los Angeles	Owns marketing company
Dave Goltz	Los Angeles	Retired
Jerry Grote	Austin, Tex.	Retired
Pedro Guerrero	Dominican Republic	Recovering from a stroke
Burt Hooton	Corpus Christi, Tex.	Fort Wayne Tin Caps pitching coach
Jay Johnstone	Pasadena, Calif.	Owns marketing company
Ken Landreaux	Los Angeles	MLB Youth Academy coordinator
Davey Lopes	San Diego	Semi-retired
Candy Maldonado	Humacao, Puerto Rico	Part-time coach
Mike Marshall	Stanford, Calif.	Ass't coach New Mexico Highlands University
Bobby Mitchell	Salt Lake City, Utah	Yankees' Double-A coach

Name	Location	Role
Rick Monday	Vero Beach, Fla.	Dodgers' broadcaster
Tom Niedenfuer	Sarasota, Fla.	Retired
Alejandro Pena	Dominican Republic	Retired
Jack Perconte	Lisle, Ill.	Baseball instructor/author
Ted Power	Los Angeles	Cincinnati Reds' bullpen coach
Jerry Reuss	Las Vegas, Nev.	Broadcaster/photographer
Ron Roenicke	Los Angeles	Red Sox's bench coach
Bill Russell	Los Angeles	Umpire observer for MLB
Mike Scioscia	Los Angeles	Los Angeles Angels' manager
Reggie Smith	Encino, Calif.	Runs baseball academy
Dave Stewart	San Diego	Player agent
Rick Sutcliffe	Los Angeles	ESPN broadcaster
Derrel Thomas	Riverside, Calif.	Part-time baseball coach
Fernando Valenzuela	Los Angeles	Dodgers' broadcaster
Steve Yeager	Los Angeles	Retired
Gary Weiss	Brenham, Tex.	Retired

In memoriam, lest we forget: Steve Howe died April 28, 2006; Bob Welch died June 9, 2014; Bobby Castillo died June 30, 2014.

*Compiled by Danny Gallagher with help from Dodgers players and personel.

promoting their clients. That was the heyday of late-night television, with the king himself, Carson, leading the way. To put things in perspective, *The Tonight Show* had begun in 1962 and was a leading late-night staple for 30 years. "H-e-r-e-e-'s Johnny!" was the lead-in, bellowed by announcer Ed McMahon, and what followed was a big-band blast led by Doc Severinsen and his trumpet. Eventually, Carson would come on and start the show with a monologue.

"Doc Severinsen heard us rehearsing and he fell on the floor laughing because we had no talent," Monday said, chuckling. "I had played golf with Doc before that. Then we went on live, we were attempting to sing, and I looked over and saw Carson laughing so hard he fell over his chair. When we finished singing, we went over to the chairs and started talking with Carson. He said we were terrible."

Of course, none of the four complained. They just laughed, content that they had been on with Carson, even though their talents were akin to bad karaoke singers. Reuss said,

> With regard to who was responsible for the four of us combining our lack of talent, I seem to recall that it was Jay who had first contact with Bob Emmer, an attorney at Rhino Records, who shopped the record deal for us. It was Emmer, who I interviewed a few years ago for my book, who mentioned he had business dealings with Jay before contacting him about the record. Maybe Jay contacted Rick prior to Steve and me about the Wrecking Crew project. All of this happened over 36 years ago, so my memory may be a bit hazy.
>
> Were the four of us close during our playing days? I guess that depends on how you define close. When Rick and I lived in Orange County, we would often carpool, either together or with Burt Hooton and Steve Russell, who also lived nearby. Jay and Yeager once roomed together in spring training. I'm not certain about the rooming arrangements with Rick and Steve during their playing days. Whatever the details, I still remember how much fun that off-season was.

On November 7, the Big Blue Wrecking Crew appeared on the *Solid Gold* show, where they were introduced by hosts Marilyn McCoo and Andy Gibb. In that spiel lasting four minutes and 53 seconds, the four Dodgers sang and danced and eventually flung their tops and ties to the floor to reveal T-shirts that read The Big Blue Wrecking Crew.

"That was a crazy winter for us," Reuss told me. "We took advantage of our 15 minutes of fame. I have a copy of the *Tonight Show* appearance, but I haven't released it to anyone other than Rick, Steve, and Jay, as it's copyrighted material."

But celebrity and fame didn't stop there. Later in the month, the Dashing Four appeared on the *Merv Griffin Show* (November 21) and then on the *Mike Douglas Show* (date unknown).

"Norm Crosby was the opening act on the *Merv Griffin Show*," Monday recalled. "I knew Norm from him being around Dodger Stadium. So we went in to Norm's dressing room and he said, 'I offer you condolences.' I said, 'What?' He had obviously gone into the tank because he said we could sing his opening act."

There was at least one hilarious part to the *Merv Griffin Show* appearance that took place at Disney World amusement park. "It's been so long that I don't recall much about the appearance other than the fact that Jay was missing from the stage before the show and nobody could find him," Reuss said. "While visiting with Merv, the three of us saw Jay in the second deck of the theatre, pants down, mooning us."

You just have to agree: Monday, Reuss, Johnstone, and Yeager did have a lot of fun.

Part Seven

AFTER ALL THAT

Chapter 36

A Special Tribute to Three 1981 Expos

GARY CARTER (THE KID)

Elected Canadian Baseball Hall
of Fame, St. Marys, Ontario, 2005
Elected National Baseball Hall of Fame,
Cooperstown, N.Y., 2003

When Gary Edmund Carter was in high school, he caught the eye of Expos signing scout Bob Zuk, who would actually hide behind trees during high-school and later college games in California so that the other scouts wouldn't notice his zeal for the player. Eventually, Zuk got his man.

The legendary Expos catcher was drafted by Montreal in 1974 as a shortstop. Then he was trained as an outfielder, but he ultimately became a star behind the plate.

When Carter first arrived, teammates like first-baseman Bob Bailey sat up and took notice. "I'll tell you, when Gary Carter came up, he was a 'can't miss' star. This kid had it all," Bailey recalled in 2017.

"We did a lot of drills together," said Tom Wieghaus, who had a cup of tea with the Expos in 1981 and 1983. "We were all good catchers and could hold

WHERE ARE THE 1981 EXPOS NOW?*

Player	Where he resides	What he is up to
Stan Bahnsen	Boca Raton, Fla.	MSC Cruises promoter
Dan Briggs	Worthington, Ohio	Big League Baseball School
Ray Burris	Clearwater, Fla.	Phillies' rehab pitching coach
Warren Cromartie	Miami	Broadcaster 6 months per year in Japan
Andre Dawson	Miami	Co-owner Grace funeral home in Miami
Rick Engle	Batavia, Ohio	Unknown
Terry Francona	Tucson, Ariz.	Cleveland Indians' manager
Mike Gates	Simi Valley, Calif.	Painter on movie/TV sets last 30 years
Tom Gorman	Oregon City, Ore.	High-school pitching coach
Bill Gullickson	Palm Beach Gardens, Fla.	Fishing and golfing
Tommy Hutton	Palm Beach Gardens, Fla.	Part-time broadcaster
Grant Jackson	North Florida	Retired
Anthony Johnson	Memphis, Tenn.	Unknown
Wallace Johnson	Gary, Ind.	Certified accountant
Dave Hostetler	Dallas, Tex.	Riddell helmet salesman
Bill Lee	Craftsbury, Vt.	Analyst TSN 690 Radio in Montreal
Brad Mills	Exeter, Calif.	Cleveland Indians' bench coach
Willie Montanez	Puerto Rico	Retired
Rowland Office	Sacramento, Calif.	Working in youth baseball
David Palmer	Glens Falls, N.Y.	High-school pitching coach
Bob Pate	Carson, Calif.	Salesman Keller Williams Realty

Name	Location	Status
Larry Parrish	Fort Gaines, Ga.	Hobby farmer
Mike Phillips	Irving, Tex.	Salesman for various corporations
Jerry Manuel	Sacramento, Calif.	Promoting black players in baseball
Tim Raines	Goodyear, Ariz.	Ambassador for Jays and White Sox
Steve Ratzer	Bluffton, S.C.	Coach Batters Box Batting Cages
Jeff Reardon	Palm Beach Gardens, Fla.	Watching grandchild grow up
Steve Rogers	Tulsa, Okla.	MLBPA special assistant
Bobby Ramos	Miami	Retired
Pat Rooney	Chicago	Player agent for SFX Sports
Scott Sanderson	Northbrook, Ill.	Retired
Rodney Scott	Indianapolis, Ind.	Semi-retired
Bryn Smith	Santa Maria, Calif.	High-school pitching coach
Chris Smith	Japan	Lived there since 1995
Elias Sosa	Scottsdale, Ariz.	MLB Int'l scouting coordinator
Chris Speier	Southern Calif.	Looking for another MLB coaching job
Ellis Valentine	Grand Prairie, Tex.	Addictions counsellor
Tim Wallach	Yorba Linda, Calif.	Miami Marlins' bench coach
Jerry White	Hercules, Calif.	Watching grandchildren grow up
Tom Wieghaus	Grant Park, Ill.	Hobby farmer

In memoriam, lest we forget: John Milner died Jan. 4, 2000; Woodie Fryman died Feb. 4, 2011; Charlie Lea died Nov. 11, 2011; Gary Carter died Feb. 16, 2012.

*Compiled by Danny Gallagher with help from Expos players and personnel.

our own defensively, but offensively, Gary was so much better. If you were doing something wrong, he'd tell you. He was a class act, a really nice guy."

At one time, Bobby Goodman was a highly prized prospect with the Expos and some said he boasted more potential than Carter. Goodman had been taken fifth overall in the first round in 1972 from Bishop Byrnes High School in Memphis, Tennessee. But he peaked at Triple-A and never made it to the majors. Carter and Ellis Valentine were taken out of the same 1972 draft.

"Goodman was really good, he was outstanding. He could really hit," Expos scouting assistant Bill MacKenzie said. "But he was an accident waiting to happen. You hardly ever saw him healthy. He was walking under a dark cloud. He was warming up one time in the bullpen and he got hit in the back of the head. He was running into second one time and the ball hit him in the back of his head.

"One time when he was in Quebec City, he was in his apartment with his catcher's mitt trying to fix it with an ice pick. The ice pick was in the webbing of his mitt and somehow got knocked off the mitt and stuck in his chest. He had to call 911 to get the pick out," MacKenzie said, trying not to laugh too hard.

Goodman faded into the sunset and became a Tennessee state trooper, while Carter wound up in both the Canadian and Cooperstown halls of fame.

Carter was very popular with his teammates. He used to joke around with his good friend Warren Cromartie in the clubhouse all the time, with the two poking fun at each other. "Carter was pretty much the mood maker," Cromartie said. "He was a character. We'd give him shit for that. He'd call up to the press box because he didn't like his passed balls. We ribbed him a lot.…"

Catching coach Norm Sherry tutored Carter from 1978 to 1981. "That's what I was there for," Sherry told me. "I spent the whole time with him, like I was his shadow. He was probably tired of me. Everywhere he went, I went with him. I'd tell him how I did things and showed him how to use his hands, use his signs, and move his body. He worked hard at it."

Carter thought so much of MacKenzie, another of his mentors, that when the catcher extraordinaire was elected into the Baseball Hall of Fame in 2003, he mentioned the Canadian-born MacKenzie in his speech.

"I want to thank Bill MacKenzie, who taught me all of the fundamentals of catching," Carter said.

MacKenzie was a catcher who spent time with the Expos' Single-A team in West Palm Beach in 1969 before joining the organization as an administrative scouting assistant and coach. MacKenzie took Carter as a greenish backstop and helped him hone the skills that made him one of the best in the major leagues.

"I dealt with a lot of Expos players as they came up through the system, but Gary was my favourite," MacKenzie said proudly. "I got closer to him because of the position he played. Even when it was dark, Gary wanted me to help him out."

There were others who came to admire Carter, guys like scouting director Mel Didier, and Jack Damaska, a teammate of Carter's in Quebec City Double-A ranks. Didier was one of the first baseball executives to introduce football blocking sleds to tutor catchers such as Carter and other position players.

"Gary was a tough dude. You could tell he was going to be a good player. He was always so positive," Damaska said.

When Gary Carter died on February 16, 2012, the hearts of many Canadians were at half-mast, their eyes at half-mist.

ANDRE DAWSON (THE HAWK)

Elected Canadian Baseball Hall of Fame, St. Marys, Ontario, 2004

Elected National Baseball Hall of Fame, Cooperstown, N.Y., 2010

Andre Dawson was about as intense a baseball player as you could ever find. And much respected.

Former Expos majority-owner Charles Bronfman doesn't have to think long before telling who his favourite Expos player was. "Andre Dawson," he said. "I think he helped Warren Cromartie, he helped Tim Raines. He was an amazing player with an amazing disposition. He was the kind of person others looked up to. He wasn't a showboat. He had a lot of knee problems but he never complained."

When I asked Steve Ratzer, one of Dawson's teammates in both Lethbridge, Alberta, and Montreal, who his favourite amigo was, he was quick to mention Dawson, calling him "probably the most unique, classiest individual." He continued: "We broke in together in rookie ball in Lethbridge. He was a 12th-round pick and I was an undrafted free agent. I had a pretty good year in the league in Lethbridge that year and Andre tore it up. We became good friends that year. He's the guy I keep in touch with because we participate in alumni events."

Dawson played at Southwest High School in his hometown of Miami and was taken by the Expos in the 11th round of the 1972 June amateur draft, out of Florida Agricultural & Mechanical University, Florida A&M, an all-black institution in Tallahassee.

By 1977, Dawson was a regular with the Expos and was voted Rookie of the Year in the National League.

"Andre was my roommate in Montreal," outfielder Jerry White said. "I'd have to say he's the best guy I cherished from my days with the Expos. I used to cook a lot with him. We did a lot of cooking exercises. Andre was the best cook in the world."

Along the way, Miami buddy Warren Cromartie entered Dawson's tight circle of friends. "There's no doubt the impact he has been in my life, coming up together through the Expos' minor-league system," Cromartie said. "Born and raised in Miami, like myself, it was great being a part of the best outfielder in baseball and playing with him every day and making me better as a player and human being. Most importantly, I'm very proud to have played with him and watch him grow into a Hall of Famer and being so close to him. He's the big brother I never had. Although he is a quiet person and I am an animated personality, it was fun growing up and being a major-league player with him."

For more than 15 years, Dawson was a goodwill ambassador for the Miami Marlins but was let go in 2017 when new ownership headed by Derek Jeter took took over from the Jeffrey Loria regime.

No longer with the Marlins, Dawson spends more of his free time as co-owner of the Grace Funeral Home in North Miami, Florida, a gig he has held for close to 10 years.

TIM RAINES (ROCK)

Elected Canadian Baseball Hall of Fame, St. Marys, Ontario, 2012

Elected National Baseball Hall of Fame, Cooperstown, N.Y., 2017

Andre Dawson has friends like Warren Cromartie and Ellis Valentine — and then there's Tim Raines: Friend Number 1. "Him and I gravitated to each other," Dawson told me. "Cromartie and Valentine are close but Tim and I go way above and beyond them. We share a special bond. He's very likeable and lovable."

When the fun-loving Raines tried to crack Dawson's hard-nosed psyche and break into his hard-to-enter inner circle of friends in 1981, Dawson didn't know what to think. It took time for them to connect and bond.

By 1982, when Raines had gone on a cocaine binge, it was Dawson who took him under his wing and helped get him straightened out and off the narrow edge of foolishness.

In his Cooperstown induction speech, Raines told the audience about the many times when Dawson would take offence at some of his playfulness, and even admitted that Dawson once bashed him over the head.

"He always had a smile on his face," Dawson told me. "I never saw him play baseball. I saw him in a football video. He was sensational as a running back."

Raines went on to become a star player for the Expos for a decade before he was traded, in December 1990, to the Chicago White Sox. His stock had diminished in Montreal by then. Dave Dombrowski, the Expos' GM at the time, told me two years ago that Raines just wasn't living up to his capabilities and that it was an appropriate time to trade him.

That was the other time that Dombrowski traded a future Hall of Famer. He had also dispatched Randy Johnson to the Seattle Mariners, along with fellow pitchers Brian Holman and Gene Harris, in exchange for veteran Mark Langston. Johnson would go on to win five Cy Young Awards. Raines would win two World Series with the New York Yankees.

"The first time I saw Tim, he looked like a football player with his build," Cromartie recalled in our interview. "When I saw him run, I thought we had finally found our leadoff man. I was also happy he was from Florida. He was a great teammate, a joker in the clubhouse."

Yankees star Derek Jeter has often commented on how Raines tutored him that first season in 1996 when both started playing for the Yankees.

This brings us to a funny story about Raines's time in New York — off the field.

Raines's marketing agent Randy Grossman chuckles as he relates it: "There was this guy Leo Caputo who had a car dealership in New York. He gave cars to probably a third of the players. On opening day in 1997 the Yankees were in Seattle, and Caputo called me to see if I could leave four tickets for him. I told him my four tickets were being used. I said sorry and told him he would have to give more advance notice.

"So the Yankees fly back to New York late … from Anaheim after the road trip was over and Caputo had screwed the players. His assistant told the players they wouldn't have cars for that year. They had no cars waiting for them. But Tim had a car from Globe Motors waiting for him and he drove off … with a Mercedes, and Jeter and the guys are scrambling for cars and looking at him driving off and saying, 'What the heck?' Tim ended up doing a commercial for Globe Motors, driving around in a convertible."

Almost 20 years later, in July 2015, Raines, Dawson, Carter, and Vladimir Guerrero were selected as the Franchise Four of the Expos organization — a tremendous honour. More than 25 million fans around the world cast votes for the "Franchise Four" of each major-league team.

The results were released for each franchise's top eight players. In the case of the Expos, Steve Rogers, Dennis Martinez, Rusty Staub, and Ryan Zimmerman of the Nationals, the successor of the Expos, rounded out the top eight.

Guerrero, even though he was signed and developed by the Expos and played a good portion of his career in Montreal, did not go into Cooperstown wearing an Expos logo on his plaque. He decided to wear an Angels halo.

But at least three stars from the 1981 Expos are in Cooperstown with Expos logos on their plaques: Carter, Dawson, and Raines.

Epilogue

The Return of Baseball
to Montreal?

When Gary Carter died in February 2012, just before spring training began that year, 1981 Expos stalwart Warren Cromartie was devastated.

Cro and "The Kid" had been friends during their Expos years and afterward, so Cromartie was more than willing to help organize a number of galas, reunions, and fundraising events in aid of Carter's charitable foundation, which is based in West Palm Beach, and also for a hospital in Montreal. The first event, in June of 2012, featuring the 1981 Expos team, raised $20,000 for those causes.

Cromartie has another cause he cares deeply about; but this one involves a long-range plan: he has been working hard for years to bring big-league baseball back to Montreal.

"When I went back to Montreal in 2011, I did not see anything anywhere that indicated the Expos ever had been there," Cromartie said in an interview. "It was a complete travesty, with the history we have. Roberto Clemente played in Montreal, Jackie Robinson. There is a lot of baseball history there, so I decided to take the bull by the horns."

Although Cromartie doesn't have the money to be a primary investor, he has been beating the drums, trying to raise the capital for bringing a team back to Montreal. Several prominent businessmen, including lawyer Mitch Garber and Stephen Bronfman, son of former Expos majority-owner Charles Bronfman, have stepped up.

Cromartie figures the only way to secure a major-league team is to acquire an existing franchise and move it. There is also the issue of a new ballpark, which would be necessary to get the MLB commissioner's office interested.

Major league baseball back in Montreal some day?

Expos fans were very curious to read media accounts of a Conference Board of Canada report on how the game could possibly return to the city that had hosted the Expos for 36 seasons before they were transferred to Washington, DC, after the fall of 2004. The report was something that made Cromartie's ears perk up.

I found it interesting that the Conference Board of Canada, a federal government think-tank based in Ottawa, would weigh in on this issue. The report surmised that Montreal may have the necessary market conditions to become the home city to another MLB franchise.

Over the course of the last few years, MLB commissioner Rob Manfred has warmed up to the idea of a team returning to Montreal. For the better part of a year, Manfred has been preaching that expansion will not take place until the Tampa and Oakland lease situations have been rectified. "We're always monitoring potential markets and we are constantly updating information. Montreal is on the list," Manfred told me.

"We are Number 1. We're the ones making the most noise," Cromartie said. "We just have to wait our turn. Things are going to take their course. It might be good for a new commissioner's legacy if there was expansion or if he did something to help us to get our game back."

When asked if he would prefer a National League team or an American League team, Cromartie said: "I prefer a team."

Bronfman and prospective partner Mitch Garber met with Montreal mayor Valérie Plante in April, 2018, to discuss steps related to the building of a new stadium in downtown Montreal. Manfred has said that he prefers a new stadium be built and that he would prefer the Olympic Stadium never be used if a major-league team does return to Montreal. "We don't want to go back to Olympic Stadium," he said.

Helping Cromartie, Garber, and Bronfman beat the drums in support of a new Montreal franchise is what ExposNation (a grassroots organization spearheaded by Matthew Ross), fundraising ExposFest founder Perry Giannias, and many members of the media, including myself, have done over the years.

I have done my part to keep the flames burning by penning three books about the Expos since the team left town.

Acknowledgements

My life odyssey in baseball would have begun when I was 11 years old in 1962 when the Royal Canadian Legion peewee team in the Upper Ottawa Valley town of Renfrew, Ontario, heard about the pretty decent player I was in my hometown of Douglas, located about 15 miles northwest of there.

So I ended up playing for the Legion in a big tournament at the Renfrew fairgrounds. In that tournament, we were in the final game and I can't remember our opponent but I was waved home by the third-base coach to try and score and I was thrown out.

I was heartbroken. I cried because we didn't win the championship and I cried because it meant we didn't get a free, celebratory meal given by the Legion. I can relate to how Warren Cromartie got emotional after he missed third base during a Little League game back in approximately the same year and I can relate to how Cromartie felt, sobbing, after the Expos lost to the Dodgers on October 19, 1981.

In ensuing years, as I was employed in the writing field, I played competitive adult baseball for 27 consecutive seasons in various leagues in Ontario, Saskatchewan, and Quebec. I played for a team in Eganville, Ontario, then the Douglas Expos, Renfrew Red Sox, Sudbury Shamrocks,

Ottawa Alta Vista Ritches, Ottawa-Nepean Canadians, and Toronto Royals in Ontario; the Regina Red Sox in Saskatchewan; and the Dorval Royals in suburban Montreal, Quebec.

It was in Sudbury where I sat down in the lounge at the Mine, Mill, Smelter Workers Union bar located behind my residence to watch Game 5 of the NLCS between the Expos and Dodgers. The Labatt's Breweries Northern district sales manager Mickey McFadden had told me and my Shamrocks teammates that he would supply a free bus and tickets for any World Series games in Montreal. Alas, the gesture never came to pass.

It was in Montreal where my love affair with the Expos blossomed. It was there I covered the Expos for a number of media outlets as a beat writer. Jim Fanning, Tim Raines, Tim Wallach, and Bryn Smith of the 1981 Expos were still with the team when I arrived there in the spring of 1988.

And so what ensued were hundreds of stories and several books that I wrote on the franchise. This book focuses on the 1981 team, the only squad in franchise history to make the post-season. But, in essence, the book is a tribute not only to the Expos and Steve Rogers but also to the Dodgers and Rick Monday.

I had first interviewed Monday in the fall of 2016 for this book, but I needed another interview to acquire more quotes and information. I had decided to give scope, depth, and exposure to Monday. So I mailed him a nicely typed letter of 500 words, telling him what I had in mind. That was just before Christmas in 2016.

I hadn't heard from him after two months, so, with much trepidation, I called him on his cellphone. He picked up. He said my letter had sat on his office desk and he was planning to make contact. He thanked me for contacting him first. He agreed to a telephone interview, although I had hoped for a face-to-face meeting in Vero Beach, Florida, in March of 2017.

What ensued was a 75-minute chat about his baseball career. I poked questions at him and he gave me the goods. Some of those questions he didn't really want to answer, but he did. The inquisitive reporter in me kept asking questions. You will see in the book some startling revelations. I appreciate very much the time Monday gave me, considering we had never met.

The other key figure in the Blue Monday caper was Rogers, and I very much appreciated the exhausting two-hour interview he gave me on the phone. By the end of the interview, my right ear was really hot. Rogers's listening ear must have been hot, too.

There were so many other former Expos who gave me a lot of their time. I especially want to thank Larry Parrish and Jerry White for allowing me to go back and forth numerous times to them for more information and anecdotes either on the phone, through text messages or emails. Same with trainer Ron McClain. Andre Dawson, Warren Cromartie, Tim Raines, and Dave Van Horne were equally co-operative.

I can't forget Bill Lee, who sat down with me for two hours over breakfast in July of 2017 at the Sunflower Café in Springfield, New York, down the road and just a home run away from Cooperstown. For decades, Lee routinely did phone interviews with writers and authors but he has stopped doing that. Initially, Lee asked me on the phone to send him questions by email, but then we arranged to meet in person in upstate New York.

Jerry Reuss of the Dodgers was generous with his back-and-forth time, as were former Dodgers Dusty Baker and Davey Lopes and former owner Peter O'Malley. When I began talking with Baker at spring training in West Palm Beach, he shooed away a Washington Nationals publicist.

I much appreciate the time I spent doing microfilm research at the renowned Toronto Reference Library. Likewise, I am grateful to the public libraries in the Ontario communities of Bowmanville and Uxbridge, where I have lived during the last several years and where I spent considerable time doing research and pounding out chapters for this book.

Many thanks go out to Dundurn Press in Toronto for taking on my project. I am most grateful to this 45-year-old publishing institution, and I am most thankful that their acquisitions editor, Scott Fraser, saw promise in me and accepted this project. He's always been a huge Expos fan.

Thanks to Dundurn developmental editor Allison Hirst, project editor Elena Radic, copy editor Laurie Miller, proofreader Patricia MacDonald, designer Laura Boyle, and publicist Michelle Melski for their help along the way.

I thank my wife, Sherry, for her love and support during this project. Not only that, she was instrumental in helping me create all of the Excel charts you see in the book. I obtained similar help in this regard from my nephew/godson Greg Gallagher and niece Catherine Gallagher.

Sources

O ver the course of a year of writing and researching this book, I received a lot of co-operation from individuals that allowed me to form a picture of what happened in 1981. I tried to contact every player who took to the field that season for the Expos — over 40 in all. I scoured the internet and asked teammates and team personnel for contact info. I would especially like to acknowledge and thank immensely the group of interviewees listed below.

INTERVIEWS

Frank Albertson	Rodger Brulotte	Marie Fanning
Bill Atkinson	Ray Burris	Doug Fast
Bob Bailey	Dave Bustin	Don Fehr
Dusty Baker	Mark Cresse	Terry Francona
Sal Bando	Warren Cromartie	John Gallagher
Steve Brener	Jack Damaska	Steve Garvey
Dan Briggs	Andre Dawson	Bob Gebhard
Charles Bronfman	Duffy Dyer	Bill Grimshaw

Ross Grimsley
Randy Grossman
Bill Gullickson
E.J. Hansen
Russ Hansen
Roland Hemond
Dave Hostetler
Tommy Hutton
Gale Johnson
Wallace Johnson
Mike Kozak
Bill Lee
Greg Leonard
Bobby Lundquist
Bill MacKenzie
Ron McClain

Rick Monday
Ross Newhan
Rowland Office
Peter O'Malley
David Palmer
Larry Parrish
Ron Perranoski
Florence (Sue) Raines
Ned Raines Jr.
Ned Raines Sr.
Patricia Raines
Tim Raines Sr.
Steve Ratzer
Jeff Reardon
Tom Reich
Harry Renaud

Jerry Reuss
Steve Rogers
Marcia Schnaar
Rodney Scott
Norm Sherry
Bryn Smith
Chris Speier
Dave Van Horne
Ozzie Virgil Sr.
Tim Wallach
Joe West
Jerry White
Tom Wieghaus
Don Williams
Rick Williams
Bobby Winkles

BOOKS

Bronfman, Charles. *Distilled.* Toronto: Harper Collins, 2016.

Gallagher, Danny. *You Don't Forget Homers Like That.* Toronto: Scoop Press, 1997.

Gallagher, Danny, and Bill Young. *Ecstasy to Agony: The 1994 Expos.* Toronto: Scoop Press, 2014.

Gallagher, Danny, and Bill Young. *Remembering the Montreal Expos.* Toronto: Scoop Press, 2005.

Katz, Jeff. *Split Season: 1981.* New York: Thomas Dunne Books, 2015.

Keri, Jonah. *Up, Up, and Away.* Toronto: Penguin Random House, 2014.

King, Norm, ed. *Au Jeu/Play Ball: The 50 Greatest Games in the History of the Montreal Expos.* Phoenix: Society for American Baseball Research, 2016.

Kolber, Leo. *Leo: A Life.* Toronto, Montreal: McGill-Queen's University Press, 2003.

Monday, Rick. *Rick Monday's Tales from the Dodgers Dugout.* New York: Sports Publishing, 2006.

Raines, Tim. *Rock Solid.* Toronto: Harper Collins, 2017.

Snyder, Brodie. Illustrated by Aislin. *The Year the Expos Almost Won the Pennant.* Toronto: Virgo Press, 1979.

Snyder, Brodie. Illustrated by Aislin. *The Year the Expos Finally Won Something.* Toronto: Virgo Press, 1981.

Usereau, Alain. *The Expos in Their Prime.* Jefferson, NC: McFarland Publishing, 2013.

Williams, Dick. *No More Mr. Nice Guy.* Boston: Houghton Mifflin Harcourt, 1990.

NEWSPAPERS, MAGAZINES, AND WEBSITES

Associated Press
baseball-almanac.com
baseball-reference.com
Canadian Baseball Network
Le Journal de Montréal
Los Angeles Daily News
Los Angeles Times
Montreal Gazette
New York Times
Ottawa Citizen
Philadelphia Bulletin
Postmedia Network
La Presse (Montreal)
retrosheet.org
SABR BioProject
Sports Illustrated

VIDEOS/BROADCASTS

Game clips: CBC, CTV, NBC, CBS, Radio Canada

Blue Monday — Les Expos de 1981. RDS documentary, originally aired October 19, 2015. Directed by Philippe-André Moreau.

NBC News *Today Show*: October 20, 1981. Bryant Gumbel interview with Rick Monday and Tommy Lasorda.

YouTube clips and transcripts from 1981, courtesy of Major League Baseball Productions.

Image Credits

Index

Book Credits

Acquiring Editor: Scott Fraser
Developmental Editor: Allison Hirst
Project Editor: Elena Radic
Copy Editor: Laurie Miller
Proofreader: Patricia MacDonald

Interior Designer: Laura Boyle

Publicist: Michelle Melski

Dundurn

Publisher: J. Kirk Howard
Vice-President: Carl A. Brand
Editorial Director: Kathryn Lane
Artistic Director: Laura Boyle
Director of Sales and Marketing: Synora Van Drine
Publicity Manager: Michelle Melski

Editorial: Allison Hirst, Dominic Farrell, Jenny McWha, Rachel Spence, Elena Radic
Marketing and Publicity: Kendra Martin, Kathryn Bassett, Elham Ali

dundurn.com   dundurnpress
@dundurnpress   dundurnpress
dundurnpress   info@dundurn.com

FIND US ON NETGALLEY & GOODREADS TOO!

DUNDURN